What Would Our Founding Fathers Say?

WHAT WOULD
Our Founding
Fathers Say?

How Today's Leaders Have Lost Their Way

H. John Lyke

iUniverse, Inc.
Bloomington

What Would Our Founding Fathers Say?
How Today's Leaders Have Lost Their Way

Data and CRP press release used by permission of the Center for Responsive Politics (OpenSecrets.org). For more information, please visit http://www.opensecrets.org.

iUniverse books may be ordered through booksellers or by contacting:

iUniverse
1663 Liberty Drive
Bloomington, IN 47403
www.iuniverse.com
1-800-Authors (1-800-288-4677)

Because of the dynamic nature of the Internet, any web addresses or links contained in this book may have changed since publication and may no longer be valid. The views expressed in this work are solely those of the author and do not necessarily reflect the views of the publisher, and the publisher hereby disclaims any responsibility for them.

Any people depicted in stock imagery provided by Thinkstock are models, and such images are being used for illustrative purposes only.

Certain stock imagery © Thinkstock.

ISBN: 978-1-4759-4414-3 (sc)
ISBN: 978-1-4759-4415-0 (hc)
ISBN: 978-1-4759-4416-7 (e)

Library of Congress Control Number: 2012915320

Printed in the United States of America

iUniverse rev. date: 09/04/2012

Special thanks is given to my friend and fellow writer Jim Syring. All I've learned about writing has come from him.

He was my editor for my first political book, *The Impotent Giant: How to Reclaim the Moral High Ground of America's Politics.*

He is an editor extraordinaire. Without his tutelage and support, his belief in my ideas and my writing ability, believing I can put a few words together in such a way that make sense, I would never have embarked on this second book.

CONTENTS

FOREWORD

We the people of the United States live in an era of great challenges both domestically and on a global scale. Some of these challenges are unique to our modern society, and some recount the familiar refrains of man's struggle as documented throughout the course of human history.

Globally, we are recent witnesses to epic natural catastrophes disrupting and indeed taking the lives of thousands of people. We shudder at reports of human rights violations, starvation, genocide, and hopelessness in distant lands. We watch live news feeds of mass demonstrations birthed by oppression and political unrest as they descend into extreme violence. Science warns of ongoing climate change and the inevitable consequences to come. Our anxieties regarding worldwide economic calamity are exacerbated by the potential of debt default by once rock-solid, major modern industrialized nations.

Domestically, we endure a sluggish economic recovery from a recession said to be the worst since the Great Depression. We struggle to find the resources to maintain and refurbish our decaying infrastructure. We are challenged with finding the funding for our educational systems and our local fire, police, and city services. Less than 1 percent of our citizens serving in the military are members of an occupying force fighting "the War on Terror" for the better part of ten years in two far-off countries. Even as we claim the designation of *the wealthiest, most powerful country the world has ever known,* a large percentage of the population dwells at or below the poverty line with scant opportunities for advancement. The promise of America—the pursuit of happiness, liberty, freedom, and justice for *all*—rings hollow for growing numbers of our disgruntled countrymen and women.

I recognize that what I've just presented is a rather dismal general summary of current events, but the good news is that we have been endowed with a system of governance capable of rising to meet the challenges of any day. It is a system unique to the world, profound in its simplicity, and empowering to all under its protections. The framework of this system constructed by our founders assures us that we have the necessary tools and the support in place to build the policies of our collective will, which will ultimately serve to confront disparities and advance the greater good.

This process of representative governance does not, however, happen automatically or without considerable struggle. The process itself requires that the members of its institutions possess the personal qualities worthy of its grand design, and it also compels the citizens who elect their representatives to perform their due diligence in assuring that those who serve are held to a standard of performance that the founders would embrace.

In *What Would Our Founding Fathers Say?*, H. John Lyke, Ph.D., offers a thorough examination of our predicament, which exposes our current government institutions as lacking the fortitude and functionality to effectively manage the challenges we face. Leveraging his lengthy career as a private practice psychologist, his tenure in the halls of academia as professor emeritus at Metropolitan State University of Denver, his experience as a detachment commander in the US Army Medical Service Corps in Korea, and his love of country and visceral sense of patriotism, John has authored a work that prompts the reader to deeply consider our nation's responsibilities to its citizens and its place in the larger world.

John establishes a strong baseline of reference for our political system by studying, analyzing, and presenting our Founding Fathers and our founding documents as the stout defenders of the idea that all men bear the right of fair and equitable representation. He conveys the concept that the genius of the Declaration of Independence, the Constitution, and the Bill of Rights is to be found in their living flexibility, which allows for relevance in modern times as cultures shift and societies advance. But this book is not just another rehashing of our founding history. John goes much further and analyzes the present state of affairs in the halls of government, offering insightful recommendations for mending our tattered national fabric.

However, in *no sense* is this a partisan tome; rather it is a call for all citizens of the nation to unite as Americans and redirect our efforts to serve our country by following the metaphorical track created by our Founding Fathers, which is sturdy and has a good foundation, *because* our Founding Fathers used as their blueprints the Declaration of Independence, the Constitution, and the Bill of Rights in its construction.

Searching for and identifying the positive qualities of character that make great leaders noteworthy, and conversely, those negative traits that engender institutional impotence, John contrasts the leaders of our nation's past with those currently serving. He identifies in our more effective leaders traits such as integrity, empathy, compassion, pragmatism, statesmanship, and honor. He contrasts those with traits used to describe a good number of today's elected officials as reflected in contemporary periodicals. The unflattering qualities that are mentioned in today's publications are such political descriptions as rigid, self-serving, greedy, intolerant, corrupt, duplicitous, uncompromising, extreme, demagogic, and/or ideological. Those expressions that describe the typical politician of today are hardly what our Founding Fathers would have envisioned or wanted our twenty-first-century politician to be described as being.

John summarizes by offering specific, *nonpartisan* remedies toward the cure of our current political and legislative dysfunction. You cannot help but agree with his diagnosis and treatment of our current condition, for his solution uses, as a template for correction, those magnificent documents, the Declaration of Independence, the Constitution, and the Bill of Rights, which together reflect the Founding Fathers' intentions for their fledging nation's character. Just by being more contemplative of our present circumstances will go a long way in engaging the reader in being part of the country's healing therapy.

I've known John for quite some time, and I recall from our conversations his fondness for a profound quote by one of his favorite philosophers,

Socrates. Socrates proposes the following: "The unexamined life is not worth living." Well, dear reader, it is high time we *examine* the state of affairs in our collective life. As this historical and political book will show, by employing the tools and framework provided us by the founders, we can endeavor to make the necessary course corrections to redirect our beloved nation toward a brighter tomorrow.

—Randy Pozniak

PREFACE

I'm H. John Lyke, Ph.D. I'm a board-certified psychologist and professor emeritus at Metropolitan State University of Denver. Prior to receiving my doctorate, I served in Korea, during peacetime, as a detachment commander in the US Army Medical Service Corps. Overseas service helped magnify my pride as an American and taught me to appreciate the uniqueness of the United States as a land of personal liberty based on laws written by and for its people.

Since my service in Korea, over time, I have observed a decay of our country's citizens' dedication to any cause greater than themselves; we have become more insular in our thinking and less willing to fight for anything if it risks putting our personal lives or treasures in jeopardy. I've also become acutely aware that millions of other Americans, although they remain silent and feel impotent and ill-equipped to initiate change of any sort, believe that our country's integrity and moral values have declined precipitously. And that transformation will be anything but what we, as citizens of this country, want and desire.

It is my belief that a sense of fairness and social justice between and among social classes and ethnic groups is much more in keeping with what our Founding Fathers had envisioned and reflected in the Declaration of Independence, the Constitution, and the Bill of Rights than what our current trend in government is reflecting. If this sense of fairness is not firmly reestablished, the government we have known will become extinct.

The governing body that will take its place will clearly not be to any law-abiding American's or Founding Father's liking.

The self-named *99 percenters,* who have recently occupied New York's Wall Street area and other city parks and prominent sites throughout this country, have spoken with a unified voice of wrath at elected officials they believe have abused our democratic system of government by *not* responding to the *common* people's needs. These protests point to the lack of legislative compromise when it comes to Wall Street's versus Main Street's concerns, and in that way, being unresponsive to the concerns of all Americans. These demonstrations represent only the tip of the iceberg of political/social revolt and unrest ahead. Unlike times past, where typically only one or a few segments of society at a time have been represented in these kinds of demonstrations—like the poor, the working classes, women, or minority groups—*now,* not only are these groups represented, but also, the unemployed young and older adults of all classes are taking a stand.

If you want to know what the 99 percenters are demonstrating about, this book is for you!

Using psychological principles, *in a nonpartisan way,* I will explain why our nation is so divided today between party lines. I will make *specific* suggestions for what needs to be done to regain our moral and political leadership as a nation so that we can each once again say, "I'm proud to be an American."

The main reason I wrote this treatise is to prevent the absolute destruction of what our Founding Fathers and fellow colonists were willing to die for to protect—which were the principles and ideals as stipulated in the Declaration of Independence, the Constitution, and the Bill of Rights.

This book is not filled with political jargon, but rather, I offer you a simple formula for fixing our political system of government. I do that by examining the events leading up to the Revolutionary War and, in so doing, help the reader understand why our *sacred* democratic documents were written, and why those superb documents continue to stand the test of time.

If we don't fix our system of government to more accurately reflect the views of all Americans, our republic as we know it today will be but a distant dream. Our democratic way of life will disappear because we failed to make the necessary changes to our Constitution to more accurately mirror our great nation's political climate, here, in the twenty-first century. For a true democracy to operate optimally, the politicians who represent the people must consider the views of *all* Americans, not just those who their political base embraces. And that's what this book is about—how to make our republic more representative, how to make our system one where all the economic classes and ethnic groups that comprise America—every one of our country's citizens—have the potential to make their dreams become a reality, where we once again can say, "I'm proud to be an American."

ACKNOWLEDGMENTS

My passion for this book wouldn't have occurred if it weren't for the able assistance of Olin Webb, Rita Herzfeld, Randy Pozniak, and my iUniverse developmental editors, Jennifer Gilbert and Kathryn Robyn. By the time my two editors and the others who assisted me did their *magic,* I couldn't help but feel like a real patriot. For it was their specific suggestions that got me more and more excited about what I was doing, as I listened to their ideas and incorporated much of what they proposed. By the time my book is published, I expect I will not only feel like a patriot, but also a Founding Father, for the process of writing these ideas has developed an ardor and deep love for what our forefathers did for our country.

It is my hope that as you read this book, you too will realize we can't take our republic for granted and, furthermore, that we must come to understand as a *people* that in order to keep our nation viable and in good health, we must use our democracy to benefit *all* Americans, regardless of their race, gender, socioeconomic levels, sexual orientation, etc. In other words, we must learn to make political compromises and pass legislation that avoids and prevents our *undemocratic* tendencies to support our biases and prejudices instead of our fellow citizens.

I owe Olin Webb, a fellow retired professor, a special thanks for diligently reviewing my manuscript and, in so doing, making specific suggestions for improving the quality and excellence of the text.

A special thanks goes to my soul mate, Rita Hertzfeld, who tirelessly reviewed my manuscript and, in so doing, made some outstanding suggestions for improving the manuscript's readability.

Randy Pozniak wrote the foreword in my first political book, *The Impotent Giant: How to Reclaim the Moral High Ground of America's Politic.* Because he captured the essence in summarizing what that book was all about and *because he represents the 99 percenters,* I asked him to write the forward for this book as well. I couldn't be more pleased with what he did.

Jennifer Gilbert, my developing editor, was upon my urging once again assigned to me by iUniverse, my book publisher. She did such a good job on my first book that I wanted her to be assigned to me again. And, as expected, she again did an outstanding job, making some exceptional editing suggestions for making my book something I was pleased to have written.

I would be remiss if I didn't mention my iUniverse content editor, Kathryn Robyn. Her depth of understanding of the subject and her compassionate and genuine interest in helping me make the book one that the potential audience would want to read was invaluable.

A postscript is indeed in order.

I recently learned I received the prestigious iUniverse Editor's Choice and Rising Star designations. Those awards would not have happened to me if it wasn't for the outstanding help that was given to me by iUniverse's very competent publication staff, all of whom shepherded me through the publication process. As a result of everyone's efforts, they all helped make *What Would Our Founding Fathers Say?* be all that it could become.

I have learned much from this whole process. Like the Founding Father's joint effort, the writing of the book was simply another example of the dedication of our team working toward something greater than ourselves and, as a result, ending up with "The whole being greater than the sum of its parts."

So, everybody who helped me on this project deserve more than a simple "thank you" from me; for what they deserve is a genuine expression of my gratitude for making this whole publication process be such a thought provoking and heartwarming experience for me, where, at the end, through our joint efforts, I was able to write something that helps us all be proud to be Americans.

CHAPTER 1

WE THE PEOPLE

Entire subdivisions of homes sit abandoned, ravaged by graffiti and the rigors of time. Squatters camp out behind the broken panes, wary of theft even though they could be seen as thieves themselves. Smoke billows from chimneys, the toxic by-product of burning anything available to stay warm. The largest alliances have claimed the shuttered libraries and universities, and will defend their territory with extreme prejudice.

Even in the wealthier parts of the city—the ones where hardly anyone has rotting teeth, badly healed broken noses, or rickets—no one ventures out at night. Many women are unwilling to walk alone even in broad daylight. Children play indoors now that stray bullets are more common and gangs have taken over the overgrown parks. Police officers are both less numerous and less trustworthy than they once were; cuts to their pay have made them more willing to take bribes in order to feed their own families. Cars and buses zoom through stoplights whenever possible; speed is safety. Those who move slowly enough to be captured will be held for ransom—or put to a variety of dark uses, if no one can afford their safe return.

Deaths from cancer, tuberculosis, AIDS, asthma, and other conditions are on the rise. For fear of contagion, the sick are often abandoned outside of town—where no one really goes anymore now that the highways are crumbling. Surgeries are often illegally performed by the lowest bidder, whether that individual has a medical degree or not: abortions, mastectomies, appendectomies …

Storekeepers shoot shoplifters on sight, an act now only illegal in the most technical sense. Wealthy subdivisions, hospitals, superstores, banks, and pharmacies are patrolled by guards in riot gear.

No, this is not a scene from your favorite dystopian science fiction novel. It's the future—or at least it might be. Let's take a brief glimpse into just a few of the issues plaguing the United States.

Mortgage Crisis

Because of the mortgage crisis, more homes are sitting empty than ever before. According to *CBS News,* in the fourth quarter of 2011, a shocking 22.8 percent of residential properties in the United States had negative equity and were considered "underwater."[1]

One individual featured on *America Underwater,* a blog dedicated to the plight of struggling homeowners, said,

> I am a single parent, and I put $225,000, my life savings, down on my home. It is now underwater by $259,000. My life savings is gone. The company I worked for closed the office due to the economy. I'm fifty-five and have been unable to find another job. I now have no job, no life savings, and no money to even move and rent, though no one will rent to someone unemployed. All of this because of the greed and stupidity of the banks. Wonder what it will be like to be homeless and penniless. Should this be my end after a lifetime of working hard and paying my bills?[2]

As more American homes sit empty, squatting is on the rise. Michael Wilson of the *New York Times* referred to squatting criminals as "the

---

1 http://www.cbsnews.com/8334-505145_162-57393615/top-10-states-for-underwater-mortgages/?tag=back.
2 http://america-underwater.tumblr.com/post/20083735475/i-am-a-single-parent-and-i-put-225-000-my-life.

flotsam of the record wave of housing foreclosures that roared through the streets like nowhere else in New York City."[3]

Neighborhood residents reported that criminals have begun to gather in empty homes. The police have noted a spike in the looting of such homes, such as the theft of copper pipes.

"[The homes] are becoming a magnet for criminal activity," said Deputy Inspector Miltiadis Marmara. He later said of the crisis, "It's destroying our quality of life here." Empty homes have been used as strip clubs, drug-packaging plants, and brothels.

One of the most notorious examples of squatting is that of Kenneth Robinson, who spent eight months living in a $340,000 home that he didn't own or rent. He even created an e-book and website about how he accomplished the feat. A judge finally ruled that the lienholder, the Bank of America, could force him out—but not before time and money was spent on the case.

With more than eleven million mortgages underwater in March 2012, many more foreclosures may be in America's future—leaving plenty of empty properties that could potentially host squatters who will cost an increasingly impoverished society even more time and money.

In 2008, when the mortgage crisis was steadily worsening, Chip Mitchell of Chicago Public Radio reported on an apartment building full of tenants who stayed on even after the owner abandoned the property. One resident, who did not give a real name, left a few burners of his gas stove on high in order to heat his apartment. He explained how he had turned the gas back on once employees of the gas company put a lock on the building's meters: "All we had to do was grab a pair of pliers, a plumbing pipe. And we just busted it out and turned everyone back on real quick … You guys are paying for the gas. Or the state or the city. I don't know who is."[4]

Anyone who might call him a freeloader might feel more empathy at his final statement in the interview: "I want to get the hell out of here

---

[3] http://www.nytimes.com/2011/10/15/nyregion/foreclosures-empty-homes-and-criminals-fill-them-up.html?ref=squatters#.

[4] http://www.wbez.org/story/news/local/mortgage-crisis-opens-doors-squatters.

and get a job. That's what I'm looking for. Whatever it takes to make an honest buck, I'd do it."

But in the United States, finding a way to make an honest buck is harder than it sounds.

Unemployment and Poverty

America is suffering its longest period of unemployment since the Great Depression, as reported by the Congressional Budget Office in February 2012.[5]

The increasing poverty of what was once the middle class has been chronicled in the media over the past several years. In 2009, *New York Times* reporter Erik Eckholm wrote of the growing number of families doubling up in residences, relying on motels, or otherwise struggling with poverty related to newfound unemployment.

"Longtime workers who lost their jobs are facing the terror and stigma of homelessness for the first time, including those who have owned or rented for years," Eckholm reported. Terry Lowe, the director of community services in Anaheim, California, told Eckholm, "People asking for help are from a wider demographic range than we've seen in the past, middle-income families."[6]

A few years later, the trend had continued. "Unlike in the 1980s," wrote *New York Times* reporter Alan Feuer in February 2012, "when the [homelessness] crisis was defined by AIDS patients or men who slept on church steps, these days it has become more likely that a seemingly ordinary family, rushing about on public transportation with Elmo bags and video games, could be without a home."[7]

The story went on to report that of New York's more than 40,000 people in homeless shelters, three-quarters were families, many of whom still got up in the morning and went to work or school. Many spoke of layoffs or reduced hours.

---

5 http://www.usnews.com/news/articles/2012/02/16/cbo-longest-period-of-high-unemployment-since-great-depression.
6 http://www.nytimes.com/2009/03/11/us/11motel.html?pagewanted=all.
7 http://www.nytimes.com/2012/02/05/nyregion/ordinary-families-cloaked-in-a-veil-of-homelessness.html?pagewanted=all.

Late 2011 and early 2012 showed a few upticks in the country's economic health, but the gains were wobbly at best, strengthening for a few months before decreasing again in March, according to the *New York Times*. "Although signs pointed to a strengthening economy earlier this year," wrote reporter Motoko Rich in April 2012, "the jobs report on Friday came with a message: don't get ahead of yourself."

Health-Care Crisis

In 2009, *Time* Magazine reported that forty-five million Americans have no health-care coverage at all. Even the insured aren't always spared the financial devastation:

> [The underinsured] may be all the more vulnerable because, until a health catastrophe hits, they're often blind to the danger they're in. In a 2005 Harvard University study of more than 1,700 bankruptcies across the country, researchers found that medical problems were behind half of them—and three-quarters of those bankrupt people actually had health insurance. As Elizabeth Warren, a Harvard law professor who helped conduct the study, wrote in the *Washington Post*, "Nobody's safe ... A comfortable middle-class lifestyle? Good education? Decent job? No safeguards there. Most of the medically bankrupt were middle-class homeowners who had been to college and had responsible jobs—until illness struck."[8]

Many middle-class Americans can continue to make ends meet as long as they remain in relatively good health—but should a true medical catastrophe occur, no amount of savings will help them. Something as simple as a broken arm can cost tens of thousands of dollars to treat—so a more serious illness can easily wipe out the maximum lifetime benefit of an insurance policy and pile tens, if not hundreds of thousands of dollars of debt on top of that. As *Time* Magazine reporter Karen Tumulty observed, (emphasis added):

---

8 http://www.time.com/time/magazine/article/0,9171,1883378,00.html.

Every story is different, but the contours of the problem tend to be depressingly similar: the 10-year-old leukemia patient in Ohio who, after three rounds of chemotherapy and a bone-marrow transplant, had almost exhausted the maximum $1.5 million lifetime benefit allowed under her father's employer-provided plan; the Connecticut grocery-store worker who put off radiation treatments for her stage 2 breast cancer because she had used up her company plan's $20,000 annual maximum and was $18,000 in debt; the New Hampshire accountant who, unable to work during his treatment for stage 3B stomach cancer, had to stop paying his mortgage to afford a $1,120 monthly premium for coverage with the state's high-risk insurance pool. *What makes these cases terrifying, in addition to heartbreaking, is that they reveal the hard truth about this country's health-care system: just about anyone could be one bad diagnosis away from financial ruin.*[9]

A discussion of the variety of medical crises that could potentially befall the average person is outside the scope of this text. But even a brief glimpse at cancer statistics alone is alarming. In January 2012, the American Cancer Society reported that half of all men and one-third of all women in the United States will develop cancer during their lifetimes.

Ah, but there's good news: "The risk of developing most types of cancer can be reduced by changes in a person's lifestyle, for example, by quitting smoking, limiting time in the sun, being physically active, and eating a better diet."[10] Of course, in a country where Congress voted to grant tomato paste a disproportionate amount of nutritional credit in school-lunch regulations to make "it easier and cheaper for pizza manufacturers to produce a product that includes a serving of vegetables," perhaps that's not so reassuring.[11]

---

[9] http://www.time.com/time/magazine/article/0,9171,1883378-2,00.html.

[10] http://www.cancer.org/Cancer/CancerBasics/questions-people-ask-about-cancer.

[11] http://www.washingtonpost.com/blogs/ezra-klein/post/did-Congress-declare-pizza-as-a-vegetable-not-exactly/2011/11/20/gIQABXgmhN_blog.html.

Obesity is a known cause of health crises, among many other causes. A January 2012 report by the National Health and Nutrition Examination Survey noted that more than a third of US adults are obese, along with approximately 17 percent of children and adolescents aged two to nineteen years.[12] "During the past twenty years, there has been a dramatic increase in obesity in the United States and rates remain high," reported the Centers for Disease Control and Prevention (CDC). "In 2010, no state had a prevalence of obesity less than 20 percent."[13]

So, just one major cause of health issues can be found in a third of the adult population—and that's just *one* major cause. Environmental carcinogens are another—and there's bad news on that front as well.

The President's Cancer Panel, a presidential advisory panel established by the National Cancer Act of 1971, said in a 2010 report that "the true burden of environmentally induced cancer has been grossly underestimated ... The panel urges you most strongly to use the power of your office to remove the carcinogens and other toxins from our food, water, and air that needlessly increase health-care costs, cripple our nation's productivity, and devastate American lives."[14]

Meanwhile, the costs of medical treatment can be staggeringly high. Genentech's Avastin, used to treat women with advanced breast cancer, costs $88,000 a year. One course of treatment with Provenge, used to treat prostate cancer, costs $93,000.[15] In a country where so many Americans can't afford a few months of unemployment, how is anyone going to afford these—and if no one can, who is going to pay for it?

America in Trouble—Again

America has survived crises before, thanks to groups of proud citizens who were willing to sacrifice everything to save it. These patriots, who lived

---

12 http://www.time.com/time/magazine/article/0,9171,1883378-2,00.html.
13 http://www.cdc.gov/obesity/data/trends.html.
14 http://abcnews.go.com/Health/Wellness/cancers-environment-grossly-underestimated-presidential-panel/story?id=10568354#.T4H9Or9AZsw.
15 http://www.nytimes.com/2011/07/07/opinion/07thu2.html.

with honor and integrity, are now known as the Founding Fathers.[16] The men and women of their era undertook enormous risks in order to build the country they wanted.

As we examine their story and compare it to our own, we face a difficult question: Are modern American citizens prepared to make those same sacrifices?

---

[16] During the writing of the Declaration of Independence, which was written about a year into the Revolutionary War, the name Thirteen Colonies was replaced with the name still used today, America.

CHAPTER 2

THE REVOLUTIONARIES

On December 19, 1777, twelve thousand men marched into Valley Forge, Pennsylvania—two-thirds of them without shoes despite the winter conditions, their marching feet leaving bloody prints in the snow. Six weeks would pass before they had shelter, and more than two thousand of them would be dead of malnutrition, typhoid, jaundice, dysentery, pneumonia, exposure to cold temperatures, and other causes by winter's end. Many ate only "fire cake," a mixture of flour and water—the very same mixture that even the poorest Americans today wouldn't use as anything but a makeshift craft paste.

Women marched in the back of the column, following the soldiers in order to serve as laundresses and nurses. Around five hundred women accompanied the troops, some of whom died on the field trying to recover goods from wounded or dead soldiers.

Of these suffering human beings, their leader wrote, "To see the men without clothes to cover their nakedness, without blankets to lie upon, without shoes ... without a house or hut to cover them until those could be built, and submitting without a murmur, is proof of patience and obedience which, in my opinion, can scarcely be paralleled."[17]

---

[17] Washington, George. "Valley Forge Encampment: A Winter of Suffering," http://www.cr.nps.gov/logcabin/html/vf.html.

That leader was George Washington, and his people were fighting in the Revolutionary War in hopes of a better America. When this war began, the citizens of the thirteen American colonies had no professional armed forces. The task of defending their rights and dreams fell onto these average people, who carried whatever armaments they could find and lacked military training. At Valley Forge and many other battlegrounds, the losses they suffered in the name of freedom were enormous.

These people sought to defend the principles that had been established in the Declaration of Independence and would ultimately shape the Constitution and Bill of Rights.

These three documents could save our country yet today.

Politicians with Integrity

On July 4, 1776, a man named Thomas Jefferson became the voice of a war. His country,[18] now envisioned as the United States of America, was fighting for its freedom from Britain, which had imposed a series of taxes and other burdens upon the thirteen North American colonies without allowing them representation in the British Parliament.

When Thomas Jefferson wrote the Declaration of Independence, a document summarizing his country's bold assertion of its rights, he knew his life was on the line. If his country lost its fight for freedom, he would be dragged to the gallows, hanged by the neck, and then cut down alive. His entrails would be taken out and burned while he was still alive. Finally, his head would be cut off, and his body divided into four parts; his head and quarters would be at the disposal of the king of England.

What prompted Thomas Jefferson to take on such an active role in the Revolutionary War that would ultimately result in the independence of the United States? Was he a lower-class vigilante with nothing left to lose, ravaged by poverty and spurred by desperation? Was he, like most of the modern-era Americans fighting for a better tomorrow, at the end of his rope with an underwater mortgage, poor educational opportunities, nonexistent health care, and a general hopelessness?

---

18 After the Declaration of Independence was signed, the name America was adopted by the revolutionaries.

Not at all. In fact, Thomas Jefferson's first memory was of being carried on a pillow by a slave. He was studying Latin, Greek, and French by the age of nine; played the violin; and graduated college with high honors. He became a lawyer who would build his own neoclassical mansion on five thousand acres of land. He would own hundreds of slaves in his lifetime (though he would fight in favor of abolishing slavery at various points during his career).

Were Thomas Jefferson a politician today, he might rest on his laurels, satisfied with a fairly cushy existence. But Jefferson was not like most of today's politicians. While as imperfect as any man, he had *political* integrity. He didn't just trumpet his principles publicly, only to forget them behind closed doors.

He was, in fact, willing to die for those principles, gutted by his enemy and decapitated for his commitment to the cause—and he wasn't the only one.

More than fifty delegates met at both the First Continental Congress and Second Continental Congress, the bodies of government that originally formed in response to British laws that cracked down on trade and levied taxes against the thirteen colonies. Among them were Samuel Adams, John Adams, Patrick Henry, George Washington, Richard Henry Lee, John Jay, and John Dickinson. All of these delegates were risking their lives, but they banded together despite their different economic, political, and educational backgrounds.

As delegate, Benjamin Franklin wryly noted during the signing of the Declaration of Independence, "Indeed we must all hang together; otherwise we shall most assuredly hang separately."

Does that sound like an attitude our Congress might espouse today?

Irreconcilable Differences

The decision to resist British domination and abuse of colonial rights and freedoms did not happen overnight. It took a number of years of thoughtful deliberation and efforts toward peace before the American colonists realized they had irresolvable differences with England that couldn't be settled short of war.

Knowing that England had a well-established army and a superior naval force at their disposal, the thirteen colonies knew the chances of winning the conflict were not in their favor. The fact that they were willing to risk all speaks to their moral obligation to free themselves from British despotism, even at the risk of failure and ultimate death.

After years of enduring legislation such as the Quartering Act, which forced colonists to board British troops; the Stamp Act, which forced colonists to use a special, taxed paper for many official documents; and the Tea Act, which levied a tax on tea without offering any representation in British Parliament in return, the colonists began to escalate the conflict.

First came the Boston Tea Party in 1773, in which Boston colonists boarded tea ships and dumped the tea into the Boston Harbor in protest of various infringements on their rights. Then came the *shot heard 'round the world,* a skirmish between local militiamen and British troops in Lexington, Massachusetts, in 1775.

With that, the Revolutionary War was on. And with the Declaration of Independence, Thomas Jefferson and his fellow delegates made their official political stand against the British government, come what may.

Next to the Constitution, Thomas Jefferson's document was and still is the most influential document in American history. An analysis of the text yields a collection of principles that remain just as relevant to Americans today:

THE DECLARATION OF INDEPENDENCE [UNEDITED]
IN CONGRESS, JULY 4, 1776.
A DECLARATION BY THE REPRESENTATIVES OF
THE UNITED STATES OF AMERICA.
IN GENERAL CONGRESS ASSEMBLED.

WHEN in the Course of human Events, it becomes necessary for one People to dissolve the Political Bands which have connected them with another, and to assume among the Powers of the Earth, the separate and equal Station to which the Laws of Nature and of Nature's God entitle them, a decent Respect to the Opinions of Mankind requires that they should declare the causes which impel them to the Separation.

Put quite simply, the Americans here are asserting their right to stand up for themselves, and to part ways with any government or other political leadership that puts human beings in the unnatural position of lacking certain rights or status.

We hold these Truths to be self-evident, that all Men are created equal, that they are endowed by their Creator with certain unalienable Rights, that among these are Life, Liberty and the Pursuit of Happiness—That to secure these Rights, Governments are instituted among Men, deriving their just Powers from the Consent of the Governed, that whenever any Form of Government becomes destructive of these Ends, it is the Right of the People to alter or to abolish it, and to institute new Government, laying its Foundation on such Principles, and organizing its Powers in such Form, as to them shall seem most likely to effect their Safety and Happiness. Prudence, indeed, will dictate that Governments long established should not be changed for light and transient Causes; and accordingly all Experience hath shewn, that Mankind are more disposed to suffer, while Evils are sufferable, than to right themselves by abolishing the Forms to which they are accustomed. But when a long Train of Abuses and Usurpations, pursuing invariably the same Object evinces a Design to reduce them under absolute Despotism, it is their Right, it is their Duty, to throw off such Government, and to provide new Guards for their future security. Such has been the patient sufferance of these Colonies; and such is now the Necessity which constrains them to alter their former Systems of Government. The History of the present King of Great Britain is a History of repeated Injuries and Usurpations, all having in direct Object the Establishment of an absolute Tyranny over these States. To prove this, let Facts be submitted to a candid World.

Here, we receive a more detailed idea of the sorts of rights and freedoms being denied the American people, including the famous tenets of life, liberty, and the pursuit of happiness. Jefferson is, in no uncertain terms, stating his people's willingness to fight for their independence from tyranny. Specifically, the king of Great Britain is named as an authority figure who has abused his power over the American people. Jefferson goes on to list those abuses—a whopping twenty-seven of them:

> He has refused his Assent to Laws, the most wholesome and necessary for the public Good.

The king has refused to ratify laws designed to further the well-being of society as a whole.

> He has forbidden his Governors to pass Laws of immediate and pressing Importance, unless suspended in their Operation till his Assent should be obtained; and when so suspended, he has utterly neglected to attend to them.

The king inhibited or neglected legislation in the colonies, sometimes for years. He ordered the governors of each colony to suspend laws passed by the colonial assemblies until he approved them—only to fail to do so.

> He has refused to pass other Laws for the Accommodation of large Districts of People, unless those People would relinquish the Right of Representation in the Legislature, a Right inestimable to them, and formidable to Tyrants only.

The British government viewed representation in the colonies as a privilege offered by the king, while colonists saw governing themselves as a right. In New Hampshire, South Carolina, and New York, for instance, assemblies of representatives elected by colonists were disallowed by King George III.

He has called together Legislative Bodies at Places unusual, uncomfortable, and distant from the Depository of their public Records, for the sole Purpose of fatiguing them into Compliance with his Measures.

Jefferson is alluding to the colonial governors' practice of moving assembly sites to less convenient locations, supposedly for safety reasons. Colonists felt this interfered with their ability to conduct public business, as these relocations put meetings farther away from the site of public records needed to inform meeting attendees.

He has dissolved Representative Houses repeatedly, for opposing with manly Firmness his Invasions on the Rights of the People.

The king occasionally disbanded representative bodies in the colonies, especially those that criticized the king for infringing on the rights of the colonists. The governors of the colonies would dissolve such assemblies until statements against the king were retracted.

He has refused for a long Time, after such Dissolutions, to cause others to be elected; whereby the Legislative Powers, incapable of Annihilation, have returned to the People at large for their exercise; the State remaining in the mean time exposed to all the Dangers of Invasion from without, and Convulsions within.

When an assembly was dissolved, the colonists' future attempts to elect legislators or conduct representative meetings would often be thwarted. The American people continued to press for representation, despite these attempts to quash their self-governance.

He has endeavoured to prevent the population of these States; for that Purpose obstructing the Laws for Naturalization of Foreigners; refusing to pass others to encourage their Migrations hither, and raising the Conditions of new Appropriations of Lands.

King George sought to control the flow of immigrants into the colonies, out of concern that the British population would shrink. He made it more difficult to obtain land, which offended Americans who prided themselves on their ability to use property to support their families. The king claimed the land of the colonists as *his,* despite his lack of labor on that property.

He has obstructed the Administration of Justice, by refusing his Assent to Laws for establishing Judiciary Powers.

The North Carolina legislature passed a law seeking to establish a judicial system. The British government, however, saw judicial proceedings as exclusive to the sovereign power. North Carolina, South Carolina, and Pennsylvania were forced to do without courts of law. Meanwhile, the punishment of criminals in the colonies was sorely needed in order to protect individual Americans from harm.

He has made Judges dependent on his Will alone, for the Tenure of their Offices, and the Amount and Payment of their Salaries.

Jefferson sought to separate judiciary powers from executive powers, as the current system left colonial judges at the mercy of the king's whims.

He has erected a Multitude of new Offices, and sent hither Swarms of Officers to harass our People, and eat out their Substance.

The British government had established military courts in the colonies in order to crack down on smuggling and ensure that trade laws were enforced. None of these court officials had been approved by colonial legislatures.

> He has kept among us, in Times of Peace, Standing Armies, without the consent of our Legislatures.

English troops occupied the colonies even after the Seven Years' War with France had ended. Worse, the Quartering Act required colonists to provide housing and provisions for these soldiers. Most colonies had done this during wartime, but they objected to being forced to do so in peaceful conditions. No such occupation had occurred before the Seven Years' War, so colonists questioned its necessity at this time.

> He has affected to render the Military independent of and superior to the Civil Power.

The king sought to use military power to reduce the self-governing powers of the colonies. One would expect the military to *support* the efforts of a legislative body, not inhibit it.

> He has combined with others to subject us to a Jurisdiction foreign to our Constitution, and unacknowledged by our Laws; giving his Assent to their Acts of pretended Legislation:

The *others* referred to here are the members of Parliament, who had worked with the king in order to suppress the rights of the colonists. The king did not veto the efforts of Parliament, instead giving his assent to parliamentary acts that did not address the colonists' best interests. The colonists did not feel they had consented to being governed by Parliament, even if they acknowledged themselves as British citizens who answered to King George as their commander in chief.

> For quartering large Bodies of Armed Troops among us:
> For protecting them, by a mock Trial, from Punishment for any Murders which they should commit on the Inhabitants of these States:
> For cutting off our Trade with all Parts of the World:

The above lines refer to what colonists called *The Intolerable Acts* or Parliament's response to the Boston Tea Party. Angered by the rebellious escapade, the British Parliament passed the Coercive Acts in 1774.

The first of several laws was the Boston Port Bill, which closed that city's harbor until restitution was made for the destroyed tea. Only food and firewood were permitted into the port.

Second, the Massachusetts Government Act abrogated the colony's charter of 1691, reducing it to the level of a crown colony, and substituted a British military government and forbade town meetings without the British Parliament's approval.

The third punishment was the Administration of Justice Act, which was aimed at protecting British officials charged with capital offenses during law enforcement by allowing them to go to England or another colony for trial.

The fourth Coercive Act included new arrangements for housing British troops in occupied American dwellings, thus reviving the indignation that resulted from the earlier Quartering Act, which had been allowed to expire in 1770.

For imposing Taxes on us without our Consent:

The principle of *no taxation without representation* was very important to the colonists. The Stamp Act of 1765 forced colonists to use stamped paper for many of their printed materials. This embossed revenue stamp was required to appear on legal documents, magazines, newspapers, and so forth. The law was intended to generate revenue to pay for troops housed in the colonies. Meanwhile, the colonists had no representation in Parliament, and thus no influence over how such taxes were applied.

For depriving us, in many Cases, of the Benefits of Trial by Jury:

For transporting us beyond Seas to be tried for pretended Offences:

This was an especially sore spot for colonists. Someone facing murder charges stemming from the repression of a riot or the enforcement of revenue laws could be whisked off to England for trial, rather than facing the consequences in the colonies. Similarly, Americans could be transported to England to stand trial for damaging the king's property, from military equipment to boats.

> For abolishing the free System of English Laws, in a neighbouring Province, establishing therein an arbitrary Government, and enlarging its Boundaries, so as to render it at once an Example and fit Instrument for introducing the same absolute Rule into these Colonies:
>
> For taking away our Charters, abolishing our most valuable Laws, and altering fundamentally the Forms of our Governments:
>
> For suspending our own Legislatures, and declaring themselves invested with Power to legislate for us in all Cases whatsoever.
>
> He has abdicated Government here, by declaring us out of his Protection and waging War against us.

The above passage is fairly self-explanatory—it continues to outline the colonists' frustration at being governed without their consent, and at having their own efforts to legislate themselves thwarted by Britain.

> He has plundered our Seas, ravaged our Coasts, burnt our Towns, and destroyed the Lives of our People.
>
> He is, at this Time, transporting large Armies of foreign Mercenaries to compleat the Works of Death, Desolation, and Tyranny, already begun with circumstances of Cruelty and Perfidy, scarcely paralleled in the most barbarous Ages, and totally unworthy the Head of a civilized nation.

King George considered the colonists to be in rebellion against Britain. By this point in time, British troops had torched several American towns, and the colonists' entire self-established legislature was under attack. The war against the colonies was on.

> He has constrained our fellow Citizens taken Captive on the high Seas to bear Arms against their Country, to become the Executioners of their Friends and Brethren, or to fall themselves by their Hands.

Jefferson is referring to a law passed by Parliament in December 1775 that empowered the British navy to interfere with trade between the American colonies and other countries. The British navy was authorized to capture the ships and cargoes of these other countries, and could even compel those captured to fight for the British, even in cases where the captives would be fighting against their own people.

> He has excited domestic Insurrections amongst us, and has endeavoured to bring on the Inhabitants of our Frontiers, the merciless Indian Savages, whose known Rule of Warfare, is an undistinguished Destruction of all Ages, Sexes and Conditions.

In order to weaken the colonies, the British had stirred up domestic tensions, such as those between the colonists and their slaves and between the colonists and the Native American population. The governors of the various colonies encouraged slave uprisings, and the commander of the British troops stationed in America encouraged Native American tribes to attack the colonists. (In the original draft of the Declaration, Jefferson also criticized the king for failing to suppress slave trade to the colonies, as he saw slavery as a "cruel war against human nature itself, violating its most sacred rights of life and liberty in the persons of a distant people who never offended him," but Congress removed the passage from the final version because Georgia and South Carolina did not want to end slave trade with Africa.)

> In every stage of these Oppressions we have Petitioned for Redress in the most humble Terms: Our repeated Petitions have

been answered only by repeated Injury. A Prince, whose Character is thus marked by every act which may define a Tyrant, is unfit to be the Ruler of a free People.

Nor have we been wanting in Attentions to our British Brethren. We have warned them from Time to Time of Attempts by their Legislature to extend an unwarrantable Jurisdiction over us. We have reminded them of the Circumstances of our Emigration and Settlement here. We have appealed to their native Justice and Magnanimity, and we have conjured them by the Ties of our common Kindred to disavow these Usurpations, which would inevitably interrupt our Connections and Correspondence. They too have been deaf to the Voice of Justice and of Consanguinity. We must, therefore, acquiesce in the Necessity, which denounces our Separation, and hold them, as we hold the rest of Mankind, Enemies in War, in Peace, Friends.

Put simply, Jefferson is noting the past efforts of the colonists to come to a peaceful accord with Britain. He is outlining the diligence with which Americans sought to resolve the conflict before resorting to combat. He boldly states that Britain has become an enemy, at least under wartime conditions, and concludes with a statement of the colonists' intention to fight for their independence, even at the price of their lives.

We, therefore, the Representatives of the UNITED STATES OF AMERICA, in GENERAL CONGRESS, Assembled, appealing to the Supreme Judge of the World for the Rectitude of our Intentions, do, in the Name, and by Authority of the good People of these United Colonies, solemnly Publish and Declare, That these United Colonies are, and of Right ought to be, FREE AND INDEPENDENT STATES; that they are absolved from all Allegiance to the British Crown, and that all political Connection between them and the State of Great-Britain, is and ought to be totally dissolved; and that as FREE AND INDEPENDENT STATES, they have full Power to levy War, conclude Peace, contract Alliances, establish Commerce, and to do all other Acts and Things which INDEPENDENT STATES may of right do. And for the support of this Declaration, with a firm reliance on the Protection of divine Providence, we mutually pledge to each other our Lives, our Fortunes, and our sacred Honor.

Declaration of Independence: Purpose

In the days leading up to the Revolutionary War, and even after the war commenced, there were a number of colonists who were not yet resolute about which side they wanted to be on. Did they want to stay loyal to King George III, or were they willing to risk being labeled traitors by the British government, losing everything they had, including their lives?

Ben Franklin, seventy years old, the oldest signer of the Declaration of Independence, knew what he was going to do: he was going to sign the document regardless of the consequences.

The fifty-six signers of the Declaration were an elite, enlightened group of dedicated men who were willing to do whatever it took to free their fledging nation from the jaws of British tyranny. In addition to other occupations, there were a number of lawyers, judges, merchants, plantation owners (farmers), a few physicians, several governors, as well as those who held political offices at the local legislative level. Twenty-two of the signers of the Declaration of Independence were lawyers.

John Hancock was the president of the Second Congressional Congress when it convened to debate the Declaration. His signature was first and the largest on the page. He, along with a number of signers were very wealthy. Their willingness to sign such a provocative document in spite of their wealth indicated they were willing to risk it all for something greater than themselves—for the sake of liberty.

Regardless of their financial health, all the signers did so with the understanding that once they signed, they had pledged their "lives, their fortunes, and their sacred honor." And they meant it. They were willing to give up the *illusion of security* under the British crown for a most uncertain future, which might best be characterized as chaotic, risky, and challenging.

Even once the war was won, these men would have to build a nation. And build it they did, with new documents like the Constitution and its first ten amendments, known as the Bill of Rights.

CHAPTER 3

THE CONSTITUTION AND
THE BILL OF RIGHTS

Before we talk about the Constitution and the Bill of Rights, a word about personal freedom is in order. Personal freedom is important in any form of government, whether it be a democracy or a republic. The Founding Fathers, George Washington's Continental Army, and the colonists were willing to give up their lives in their efforts to oppose British tyranny and protect their freedoms. Eventually, those personal freedoms—the individual's inalienable rights—were clearly stated in the soon-to-be-established Constitution of the United States of America.

A *democracy* and a *republic* are two forms of government that are distinguished by how the voting majority treats the minority and the individual.

In a democracy, the majority has unlimited power over the minority—neither the minority nor the individual's views or rights are legally safeguarded. The dangers inherent are frequently referred to as the *tyranny of the majority*. That's because the majority plus one, dictates policy without considering the needs and desires of the minority, whether referring to a group or an individual.

In a republic, the majority is limited and constrained by a written constitution or a charter, which protects the rights of the individual and the minority. The purpose of a republican form of government is to control the majority for the protection of the *God-given*—those *inalienable rights and liberties* of the individual and the minority. Those rights and liberties are defined in the republic's constitution or charter. The United States of America is founded as a republic under our Constitution.

Democracy involves the government ruling and making laws for the *greater good* of all people; it may abolish personal rights in so doing. Democracy is government "by and for the people." It may or may not be a republic, which, again, is limited by constitution or charter.

Republics involve the government's routinely using and abiding by its constitutions or charters. Personal rights are respected and cannot be taken away. This helps to avoid the tyranny-of-the-majority phenomenon, when the majority makes laws and governs by passion, prejudice, or impulse, without restraint or regard to consequences or the effect their governance has on a minority. Republics are the common or *standard* type of government found today, not democracies, despite what many people (who may not know the definition of either) think.

Just as democracies may or may not be republics, *republics may or may not be democracies.*

In summary, if a democracy is also a republic, the government is limited by a charter or a constitution to avoid tyranny by the majority when the majority makes laws and governs by fervor, unfairness, or whim, without moderation or regard to outcome. Hence, minority interests are protected by that charter.

If a democracy is not limited by a charter or constitution, the government might rule and make laws for the "greater good," or not, but in so doing, they may also abolish personal rights and the majority can wreak tyranny upon the minority.

In a democratic *republic,* the people elect its ruler. In a nondemocratic republic, the people who serve in government may be either plural or singular. If plural, the group only has advisory powers. A sovereign ruler is free to reject the majority advisory group's decisions, endangering the likelihood of any true representation of the needs of the people the ruler "serves." Similarly, government by the few are likely to rule in their own favor, the people be damned. Therefore, the choices made in a nondemocratic republic may or may not represent either majority or minority interests. Without recourse, there's no individual protection for perceived governmental abuses.

We do not have a true democracy, even though our government is a republic, because although the voters decide who their governmental representatives and government executive will be, those people *are* empowered to make and enforce the laws under which the rest of us are bound. We trust that our officials will represent the people's best interests when they are in Congress or become president of the United States.

It's clear that a republican form of government is preferred over a democracy, because that form provides the opportunity for freedom to survive and thrive. However, in order for freedom to serve the people in the best possible way, their representatives, the politicians, have to be willing to *compromise* with one another so that they at least partially serve the needs of *all* the people.

* * *

The Constitution was written after General George Washington and his Continental Army had won their revolutionary war. The American Revolutionary War began April 19, 1775, and ended September 3, 1783. And it certainly was *revolutionary,* because the winning of the war set the stage for groundbreaking, even *world-shattering,* conceptions of what a country's government should be all about—as spelled out by our Declaration of Independence.

That document clearly articulates why there are so many political uprisings worldwide today: It is natural for people to yearn for a government that respects their rights to be treated with respect and dignity. It is self-evident that we are all created as equals, have been endowed by *each* of our Creators "with certain unalienable Rights, that among these are Life, Liberty and the pursuit of Happiness." Those longings and beliefs provided the American colonists with the impetus and reasons to sever their ties with their mother country, England. They clearly still exist today in people all over the world. And they still exist in the United States.

After the Revolutionary War, our fledging nation's next task was to replace the British Parliament and king's tyrannical government with one more suited to protect America's freedom, which they had fought so valiantly to preserve. The Second Continental Congress was convened with delegates appointed by the legislatures of the state. Such notable Americans as George Washington, Patrick Henry, John Adams, Samuel Adams, Benjamin Franklin, John Hancock, and Thomas Jefferson, to mention but a few, were in attendance. After much discussion, they adopted the Articles of Confederation to frame a national government. The name of that government was the Congress of the Confederation (1781–1789), and this replaced the existing Second Continental Congress.

The powers of the national government, or the Congress of the Confederation, as spelled out in the Articles of Confederation, were limited in scope and power. They were empowered to declare war, negotiate treaties and alliances, regulate Indian affairs, establish post offices, raise national treasury through state contributions, and produce coin money (which many of the state governments did as well). And that was about it.

After the Revolutionary War, political power reverted back to state capitals. Because there was no central authority or overall control of the thirteen state governments, there were rumblings as early as September, 1785, that the Articles of Confederation needed to be revised.

The Congress of the Confederation had helped guide the United States through the final stages of the Revolutionary War. But during peacetime, the Congress of the Confederation proved inadequate to govern, because there was no empowered federal government to help regulate and control what the thirteen states could or could not do—in order to fairly and adequately meet the needs of all of its American citizenry.

It was then that James Madison, a protégé of Thomas Jefferson's and the youngest delegate to the Congress of the Confederation, from Virginia, expressed his discontentment to George Washington over how irresponsible the states were in managing their governmental affairs. Washington believed that in order to make the necessary changes to the

Articles of Confederation and meet the needs of their young nation, a crisis of some magnitude would need to occur.

Shays's Rebellion, an uprising of over a thousand farmers in Western Massachusetts, led by Daniel Shays in 1786 and 1787, provided that impetus. A group of protesters, driven to desperation by an economic depression, excessive debt, and foreclosures shut down county courts in order to halt hearings on tax and debt collection. The rebels even began to organize armed forces, but when they attempted to seize the federally controlled Springfield Armory in 1787, the rebellion was scattered by a militia.

While not immediately successful, Shays's Rebellion, resulted in the go-ahead to begin work on our Constitution, for which James Madison was the principal architect. For our purposes, the salient point is that, once again, a group of *citizens*—not lawyers or professors, but farmers of very modest means—risked their lives to make a difference. Their efforts ultimately led to the drafting of one of the most important documents in history.

At the time the rebellion occurred, the United States economy was in shambles. Due to the war, there was massive debt throughout the United States. Foreign investors who had aided the Patriot Army during the war started to call in their debts, and the Continental Congress had to borrow money simply to pay the accumulating interest, never mind paying anything on the principal.

The Founding Fathers recognized that, under existing law as stipulated by the Articles of Confederation, solving the economic crisis would be difficult at best. That's because each of the thirteen states was acting as a sovereign nation; consequently, there was no uniform fiscal policy between or among them. This resulted in some states having paid what was requested of them, while others could not even make the minimum amount asked. The country as a whole faced a dire situation.

Shays's Rebellion not only sparked a turnaround, but also led to the development of a group—eventually calling themselves Federalists—who worked to form a central government that could oversee the workings of the state governances.

On February 21, 1787, the Congress of the Confederation called for a constitutional convention to be held in May to revise the articles. Between May and September, the delegates met in Philadelphia and wrote what we now know as the Constitution for the United States of America, which gave considerably more power to the federal government. Washington presided over the meeting, stating that the Shays's insurrection was the reason for his own attendance. He said, "There could be no stronger evidence of the want of energy in our governments than these disorders."

Shays's Rebellion was the example cited for the need of an unprecedented and powerful central government. Called the "Virginia plan," it was a plan that Washington, a federalist with a small *f,* favored. On the opposite end of the continuum were the states' rights people, such as Thomas Jefferson, who favored state sovereignty.

At the time, the term *federalist* did not refer to a party per se, but rather, a point of view. When that term was introduced, both Washington and Madison could be called federalists, because they were for the adoption of the Constitution and lobbied vigorously for its adoption. Soon the supporters of the Constitution took the name *Federalists* and affiliated with it as a party, charging their opponents with the term *Anti-Federalists,* which they really weren't. Both groups realized the importance of a strong central government, only to a *different* limited extent.

Many of the federalists favored a *strong* central government only to a limited extent. The Anti-federalists argued that it was dangerous to place so much power in the hands of so few men, particularly when they were so far away from the people they represented. One of the ways that the Federalists could be prevented from illegally usurping those functions that may rightfully go to the states was to introduce the Tenth Amendment into the Constitution within the Bill of Rights. The Tenth Amendment declared that the powers of the federal government were few and well defined and that any powers not specifically granted to the federal government by nature, reverted to the states and to the people.

The birth of the Constitution was in response to the inadequacies of the Articles of Confederation, which was primarily in response to the lack of sufficient federal control over the thirteen state governments and too much power given to the states by the Articles. As soon as the Constitution was written, the fears reversed. Fears arose that the *federal* government would become too powerful, and as a result, state governments would be at the mercy of the central government. As a result of that dichotomous thinking, it didn't take long for two parties to be born.

In the 1790s the first two official parties were formed, the Federalists, led by Alexander Hamilton and the Democratic-Republication Party, which Thomas Jefferson founded.

The Democratic-Republication Party should not be confused with today's Republican Party which was founded in 1854. Federalism stood for a sufficiently strong central government so that the affairs of the country could be adequately managed. In contrast, Thomas Jefferson's party wanted the federal government to play as small a role as possible in the lives of Americans. From Jeffersonian thinking sprouted states' rights advocates, which today's Republicans purport to favor. The Democratic Party of today mirrors Hamilton's thinking of yesteryear, where a stronger federal government than the modern day Republicans favor is necessary to handle the needs of all Americans in today's society.

The United States Constitution

I've chosen to just discuss the preamble of the Constitution because what follows after the preamble simply reinforces what the preamble states. The preamble of our Constitution reads as follows:[19]

> WE THE PEOPLE of the United States, in Order to form a more perfect Union, establish Justice, insure domestic Tranquility, provide for the common defence, promote the general Welfare, and secure the Blessings of Liberty to ourselves and our Posterity, do ordain and establish this Constitution for the United States of America."

---

[19] Although these remarks are my own, my presentation here was prompted by the website display at usconstitution.net. That website was constructed by webmaster Steve Mount and is now run by Craig Walenta.

The Constitution was written by several committees over the summer of 1787. The preamble states why the Constitution was written.

We the People of the United States …

The preamble reflects not only what the Founding Fathers, or the delegates of the convention, believed were their hopes and dreams for their fledging country, but also, acting as delegates for *The People,* what they believed represented the views of all Americans as well.

Like the signers of the Declaration of Independence, Madison and the other framers of the Constitution were indeed an elite group. They represented what was the best and brightest America had to offer at the time. Frankly, it is quite amazing that the number of men of that caliber could be seen in one gathering; nonetheless, this diverse group of men, who had predisposed interests and agendas, was able to come to a consensus and provide America with the language tools that would assure their hard-earned freedoms, won from overcoming British tyranny, would be safe-guarded for generations to come.

They were keenly aware that they were writing this Constitution not so much for themselves, but for the common man, as reflected in the statement "We the People of the United States." The delegates wanted to make it crystal clear that the writing, was *people-made,* not handed down by a god or king, but rather, was created by *the People* of the United States.

… in Order to form a more perfect Union …

The writing of the Constitution was done as a result of realizing there were obvious and apparent Articles of Confederation deficiencies that needed fixing if the nation was to survive over time. This didn't become as apparent until after the ending of the Revolutionary War. However, as the months progressed, the Articles of Confederation's deficiencies became more and more evident. Less than ten years into the formation of the Articles of Confederation, the founders realized the document needed to be replaced by a constitution. The founders realized that their United States would be "more perfect" than before, meaning that they knew it was not perfect, but it would be closer to the ideal than before.

... establish Justice ...

Based on what the colonists had experienced when they were subjects of the British crown, injustices such as the unfairness of laws and trade were of top concern to the people of 1787. People looked forward to a nation with a level playing field, where courts were established with uniformity and where trade within and outside the borders of the country would be fair and unmolested. Although our system of justice is not by any means ideal, it is among the fairest in the world. Though discrimination continues to exist, and some citizens still do not have an equal opportunity to a fair trial under the law, there is less discrimination than existed earlier.

... insure domestic Tranquility ...

The Shays's Rebellion involved a revolt of Massachusetts farmers who had recently finished serving under General Washington during the Revolutionary War. These farmers became angry that their state government was not adequately addressing the needs and realities of those who lived in the western part of the state, favoring Boston and its surrounds in all matters while taxing the rest. The Revolutionary War debt trickled down to the farmers in rural Western Massachusetts as a *head tax*. The farmers with *the largest families* paid the greater tax, compared to the lesser tax a wealthier farmer with a smaller family had to pay, and the absence of tax to the city dwellers. Failure to pay could lead to loss of land as well as imprisonment.

Those small farmers reacted angrily because of their own crippling debts resulting from wartime losses and the exorbitant taxes they had to pay to the state government. Holding that government to the then existing Articles of Confederation, they took up arms and revolted against its militia. Because of having just won the Revolutionary War, this rise up got everybody's attention. That's because keeping the peace was on everyone's mind—the maintenance of tranquility at home was a prime concern. The framers hoped that the new powers given the federal government would empower it to prevent or address any such rebellions in the future.

… provide for the common defence …

Because of the geography of the continent, the United States was vulnerable to attack from all sides. It would have been impossible for one state to fend off attacks from land or sea by itself. At the time, Washington and the thirteen states' leaders knew that if Britain attacked again or if Spain did, no one state could adequately defend itself. And of course, with the ever-present fear of Indian attacks, the new country might very well need to present a common defense involving all or some of the states to ward off the aggressors. Considering the harsh realities of the late eighteenth century, the maxim *E Pluribus Unum* ("Out of many, one"), was certainly true.[20]

… promote the general Welfare …

The framers wanted to empower the central government body to encourage the well-being of all its citizens. They recognized that the expansion of landholdings, industry, and investment was on the horizon and that there would be many things connected with those activities that the states alone could not provide. These conditions would require the federal government to intercede to help facilitate the smooth expansion of such activities. Besides *encouragement,* there has always been debate as to how much the central government should be committed to stimulating, supporting, fostering, or upholding the welfare of all its citizens, and each era takes a different approach to that issue.

… and secure the Blessings of Liberty to ourselves and our Posterity …

---

[20] Adopted in 1782 by an Act of Congress for the Seal of the United States, *E Pluribus Unum* was the new country's de facto motto until 1956 when Congress passed an act (H.J. Resolution 396), adopting "In God We Trust" as the official motto.

Liberty is the operative word in the above phrase. It is also the general theme that runs throughout the Constitution. It was why the Founding Fathers and their fellow patriots were willing to fight in the Revolutionary War and were willing to give up their treasures and their lives for something greater than themselves. They were, indeed, fighting for their liberties, the freedom to do as they wished in all aspects of their lives as long as it was within the law of the land. That law would then be specified in the Constitution.

The other word that is just as poignant and meaningful is *Posterity.* These were men who were not only writing a framework for their generation but also for *future generations*—a point that frequently is lost in our political world today.

> *... do ordain and establish this Constitution for the United States of America.*

The final clause of the preamble invites us to return to the beginning: "We the People," for it is indeed the *people* who are ordained to establish this Constitution for the United States of America. The words *do ordain* is an expression that carries a lot of meaning. It says that the *superior authority* behind this country and the charter that structures it is *the people,* not a single person: king, emperor, or pope; and not a group of persons: lords, landowners, or priests; but *all* citizens of these United States of America.

To briefly summarize: by the framers of the Constitution strengthening the function of the federal government, they were able to be the deciding authority over states' border disputes and western land acquisitions. Without a stronger unified central government, peace could not be guaranteed. By having a strong federal government, they were able to oversee free trade among the states, quell domestic rebellions, and stand strong on the international front. The new constitution did what it was intended to do, which was to take away from the states what was duly the responsibility of the federal government and in so doing, create "a more perfect union."

The Bill of Rights: Reasons It Was Needed

George Mason, one of the original statesmen from Virginia, is best known for his refusal to sign the Constitution. The most important reason that Mason did not sign was the lack of an explicit statement outlining state and individual rights. Mason wrote the first document ever written about the US Constitution. Using a printed draft, he wrote his objections on the reverse side. His opposition played a large role in the addition of the Bill of Rights to the Constitution, guaranteeing the basic rights of every American citizen. For this reason, he is among the list of Founding Fathers.

The federalists might never have obtained ratification in several important states if they had not promised to amend the Constitution with the addition of a Bill of Rights. Most state constitutions adopted during the Revolution had included a clear declaration of the rights of all people, which is a strong indication that most Americans believed that no constitution could be considered complete without such a declaration. Mason and Patrick Henry, the patriot best known for his speech "Give Me Liberty, or Give Me Death," might have prevented ratification of the Constitution in Virginia if the Federalists had not agreed to their demands for these ten amendments.

The reason the states were so adamant about including some kind of declaration of the rights of all people in their state constitutions was because of the oppression, subjugation, and domination they experienced under the British crown and Parliament when they were English subjects. It was understandable that some congressional delegates feared that a constitution vesting power in a central government would lead to the same tyranny and oppression they had just overthrown in the war for independence. They didn't want their own federal government to be given so much control, for fear that power might be misused in their new America. So they wrote the Bill of Rights to limit government's power.

The Bill of Rights included ten amendments and was ratified on December 15, 1791. Because the framers of the Constitution knew it wasn't perfect, they wanted a means to change the Constitution *short* of a revolution, therefore, they provided a path to amend it, thereby allowing future generations to make changes that would better fit changing times.

Seventeen additional amendments have been passed since then, such as the right of various citizens to vote, the federal government's right to collect income tax, and the limitation of the American presidency to two terms. To date, we have a total of twenty-seven amendments, but the original amendments, known as the Bill of Rights were as follows:

First Amendment

Congress shall make no law respecting an establishment of religion, or prohibiting the free exercise thereof; or abridging the freedom of speech, or of the press, or the right of the people peaceably to assemble, and to petition the Government for a redress of grievances.

Second Amendment

A well-regulated Militia, being necessary to the security of a free State, the right of the people to keep and bear Arms, shall not be infringed.

Third Amendment

No Soldier shall, in time of peace be quartered in any house, without the consent of the Owner, nor in time of war, but in a manner to be prescribed by law.

Fourth Amendment

The right of the people to be secure in their persons, houses, papers, and effects, against unreasonable searches and seizures, shall not be violated, and no Warrants shall issue, but upon probable cause, supported by Oath or affirmation, and particularly describing the place to be searched, and the persons or things to be seized.

Fifth Amendment

No person shall be held to answer for a capital, or otherwise infamous crime, unless on a presentment or indictment of a Grand Jury, except in cases arising in the land or naval forces, or in the Militia, when in actual service in time of War or public danger; nor shall any person be subject for the same offence to be twice put in jeopardy of life or limb, nor shall be compelled in any criminal case to be a witness against himself, nor be deprived of life, liberty, or property, without due process of law; nor shall private property be taken for public use, without just compensation.

Sixth Amendment

In all criminal prosecutions, the accused shall enjoy the right to a speedy and public trial, by an impartial jury of the State and district wherein the crime shall have been committed; which district shall have been previously ascertained by law, and to be informed of the nature and cause of the accusation; to be confronted with the witnesses against him; to have compulsory process for obtaining witnesses in his favor, and to have the Assistance of Counsel for his defence.

Seventh Amendment

In Suits at common law, where the value in controversy shall exceed twenty dollars, the right of trial by jury shall be preserved, and no fact tried by a jury, shall be otherwise re-examined in any Court of the United States, than according to the rules of the common law.

Eighth Amendment

Excessive bail shall not be required, nor excessive fines imposed, nor cruel and unusual punishments inflicted.

Ninth Amendment

The enumeration in the Constitution, of certain rights, shall not be construed to deny or disparage others retained by the people.

Tenth Amendment

The powers not delegated to the United States by the Constitution, nor prohibited by it to the States, are reserved to the States respectively, or to the people.

With the completion and ratification of the Constitution and the Bill of Rights, the United States was on its way to becoming one of the greatest countries on earth—all thanks to ordinary citizens who stood united and fought for freedom, despite their individual differences.

"We the People," indeed. But who have those people become today?

CHAPTER 4

THE STATE OF THE UNION

Thomas Jefferson was an educated man who owned property and enjoyed a privileged existence. If he were growing up today, would he still become a man who fought for the freedom of all? Probably not. In fact, research indicates that Americans as a whole have become much more self-absorbed. Were he coming of age today, Jefferson would likely spend a lot less time penning historic documents and a lot more time uploading pictures of himself to social media sites—at the more flattering taken-from-above angle, of course.

It's easy to express frustration at the government. How many times have you felt fed up with a politician lately? How many times have you ruefully noted how corrupt, inept, and selfish government officials have become over time?

But the phrase is "We the People," not "They the Government." Thus, we must take a long, hard look at ourselves as well—the people who put those politicians in office in the first place. Well those of us who voted, anyway. Only about half of voting-age Americans actually do—and that's on a good day. The 2010 elections showed only a 37.8 percent turnout.[21]

---

21 http://www.infoplease.com/ipa/A0781453.html.

The founders cared deeply about building a better America—so deeply that they were willing to lose their lives. And they weren't the only ones. From the freezing, starving Continental Army to the desperate rebels of Shays's Rebellion, we've seen many examples of Americans making efforts to bring about positive societal change.

There is some hope for modern America as well. In the case of the Occupy movement, for instance, protestors across the country camped out in parks and faced a backlash from authorities for days, weeks, and months in order to bring attention to the uneven distribution of wealth in the United States and the issues arising from that distribution, such as the struggle of many to afford health care. The movement, which began in September 2011, lost a good deal of momentum in the winter months, but many feel that these protestors drew attention to issues that would otherwise have gone ignored by politicians.

Occupy has proved that the American people are, in fact, still capable of fighting for their country. But all the same, most Americans still seem less worried about liberty and more worried about taking the most flattering self-portrait, discussing how much money and riches they deserve in their lives, or pondering what actions will serve their egos, not their country.

This may sound cynical. But studies seem to support the idea that "We the People" have become a collection of "Me, Me, Me the Persons." According to the *Huffington Post,* one study found that the percentage of people classified as narcissists has doubled in the last thirty years—it's now up to 30 percent. Another study found a 40 percent decline in empathy among young people, wrote Dr. Jim Taylor, an adjunct professor of psychology.[22]

Certainly, the shift in societal values away from collectivism (*We're all in this together.*) and toward individualism (*You're on your own.*); away from civic responsibility (*It's my duty.*) and toward self-gratification (*It's what I want.*); and away from meaningful contributions to society (as defined by

---

[22] http://www.huffingtonpost.com/dr-jim-taylor/narcissism-america_b_861887.html.

public service and public goods) and toward personal success (as defined by wealth, power, and status) have also contributed to the cultural incitement of narcissism in which young people are presently immersed.

It's one thing to see that there is a growing percentage of narcissists in America today. But the real concern should not be the percentage of individual narcissists among us, but the issue of our society embracing and accepting narcissism as *the norm*. And that time may have arrived.

It doesn't seem farfetched to theorize that narcissism can make a society less informed. When we're busy worrying about who has the better car, hair, outfit, house, and so on, other topics receive less attention.

According to a 2011 poll, for instance, a jaw-dropping one in four Americans doesn't even know what country America declared its independence from in 1776.[23]

The older a respondent was, the more likely he or she was to respond correctly to questions like "In what year did the United States declare its independence?" Americans aged forty-five to seventy were those most likely to know the answer.

It's unsettling to compare these American citizens to those who successfully built an entire country, which ultimately became the most powerful nation in history. How long can we remain proud to be Americans if we don't know much about America to begin with?

Some citizens assume that even if they are not particularly well-versed in the principles and history of our government, anyone who could make it all the way to office is surely much more educated, responsible, selfless, and motivated toward positive change than they themselves are. That is, at least the American people have an educated, responsible federal government to do all of their political thinking for them, right?

Wrong.

A Troubled Congress

"The world is going to hell in a handbasket" has been a common sentiment throughout history and continues today—never mind that technology is

---

23 http://maristpoll.marist.edu/71-independence-day-dummy-seventeen-seventy-when/.

continually advancing to make our lives easier, or that women are still gradually improving their lot, or that black people had to sit in the back of the bus until very recently. People used to drop dead of scarlet fever, polio, and diabetes; a man beating his wife used to be more or less culturally acceptable in the United States; and children used to be too busy working to go to school. And still, many of us insist that humanity is in a decline.

In many cases, we can blame this perspective on nostalgia or a loss of innocence regarding problems that have always existed but are less frequently noticed by the young.

But in some cases, the claim that the world is going to hell in a handbasket is actually accurate. If someone were to say that the 112th Congress were the worst one ever, for example, that individual just might have a point, at least according to the experts.

Lest you think I'm being dramatic, note that Norman Ornstein, author of *The Broken Branch: How Congress Is Failing America and How to Get It Back on Track,* wrote a *Foreign Policy* Magazine piece in 2011 that analyzed the current Congress. The title? "Worst. Congress. Ever."

Ornstein wrote,

> And look what we have now: a long-term debt disaster with viable bipartisan solutions on the table but ignored or cast aside in Congress; an impasse over the usually perfunctory matter of raising the statutory debt limit placing the United States in jeopardy of its first-ever default; sniping and guerrilla warfare over two major policy steps enacted in the last Congress, health-care reform and financial regulation; no serious action or movement on climate change, jobs, or the continuing mortgage crisis; and major trade deals stalled yet again despite bipartisan and presidential support.[24]

A group of citizens once built a country based on their passion for freedom. They drafted documents still treasured today for wisdom and guidance, assembled legislatures, and pushed their way toward a

---

[24] http://www.foreignpolicy.com/articles/2011/07/19/worst_Congress_ever.

better life for all. Despite all the technology and information now at Americans' disposal, it seems safe to say that the current Congress bears little resemblance to that group of citizens.

What's wrong with today's Congress?

Partisanship, Brinkmanship, and Gridlock

In a 2010 interview with *National Journal,* Senate Republican Leader Mitch McConnell was very clear in naming the "single most important thing" he needed to accomplish in government in the coming years.

Was it about ensuring liberty for all Americans? Was it about helping his constituents pursue happiness? No. According to McConnell, "The single most important thing we want to achieve is for President Obama to be a one-term president."[25]

In 2008, Barack Obama had won the presidency, and the Republicans had been thrashed at the polls. As a result, the deep partisan conflict burgeoning for decades began to breed quickly, and McConnell was less a ringleader than a symptom of a greater disorder. Even after the 2010 elections, in which Republicans gained a great deal of ground, America's war with itself continued.

After Obama was elected, McConnell showed up for his job every day with the specific purpose of combating another politician—one who was supposed to be his partner in bettering the state of the country.

In an interview with *The Atlantic,* McConnell elaborated on this agenda:

> [Republicans] worked very hard to keep our fingerprints off of these proposals. Because we thought—correctly, I think—that the only way the American people would know that a great debate was going on was if the measures were not bipartisan. When you hang the "bipartisan" tag on something, the perception is that

---

[25] http://thinkprogress.org/politics/2010/10/25/126242/mcconnell-obama-one-term/.

differences have been worked out, and there's a broad agreement that's the way forward.[26]

Did McConnell just imply that cooperation is bad for government? Would a First or Second Continental Congress with his philosophy have been successful in building America?

The first bill to be considered in the 111th Congress—the first Congress after Obama's election—was the Public Land Management Act, a conservation measure that was generally supported by both parties; the bill would protect two million acres of parks and wilderness. The Republicans filibustered anyway, which resulted in a series of votes rather than just one: votes to end the filibuster, votes to end debate, votes to vote again, ad nauseam. Despite all of this contention, the bill ultimately passed—and it wasn't even close: the vote was seventy-seven to twenty.

Some filibustered issues, such as that of judicial nominees, were later passed *unanimously.* Can anyone deny that the American government is wasting its taxpayers' time and money when such utterly uncontroversial proposals are filibustered for *any* length of time?

As *The Atlantic* reported, the conflict within the American government had "slowed Senate business to a crawl." And the rest of the world definitely took notice of the brinkmanship between political parties, especially once a battle over the debt ceiling in 2011 nearly drove the country into default. As a *CNN* report warned on August 1, 2011,

> If the debt ceiling is not raised by Tuesday, Americans could face rising interest rates, and the value of the US dollar may drop compared to other currencies, among other problems. As the cost of borrowing rises, individual mortgages, car loans and student loans could become significantly more expensive. Some financial experts have warned that America's triple-A credit rating could be downgraded and the stock market—

---

26 http://www.theatlantic.com/magazine/print/2011/01/strict-obstructionist/8344/.

which has already fallen over the past week, in part due to lingering uncertainty over the debt talks—to crash. Moreover, the federal government will not be able to pay all its bills next month without an increase in the debt limit. Obama recently indicated he can't guarantee Social Security checks will be mailed out on time. Other critical government programs could be endangered as well.[27]

That's quite the expensive game of chicken Congress was playing—and by the time an accord was reached, damage had been done. Four days after that *CNN* report was published, the credit-rating agency Standard & Poor's indeed downgraded the credit rating of government bonds for the first time in the country's history.

The global community was, in a word, unimpressed. From Deng Yushan of China's *Xinhua*:

> When countries across the world hold their breath watching the debt negotiations between the Democrats and Republicans in Washington, they are once again "kidnapped" by US domestic politics. Given the United States' status as the world's largest economy and the issuer of the dominant international reserve currency, such political brinkmanship in Washington is dangerously irresponsible, for it risks, among other consequences, strangling the still fragile economic recovery of not only the United States, but also the world as a whole.[28]

From Alan Philips in the *National,* based in Abu Dhabi:

> While the United States is used to the spectacle of noisy squabbles in Congress, the current game of chicken at the heart of the world's leading economy is unsettling to say the least.[29]

---

[27] http://www.cnn.com/2011/POLITICS/08/01/debt.ceiling.battle/index.html.
[28] http://news.xinhuanet.com/english2010/indepth/2011-07-28/c_131015312.htm.
[29] http://www.thenational.ae/thenationalconversation/comment/only-shock-therapy-can-force-countries-to-break-debt-habit.

From the *Arab News:*

> The value of [Saudi Arabia's] investments, the value of our oil earnings and the value of our currency are all under threat as politicians in Washington grandstand for their constituents and argue bitterly from two utterly polarized positions.[30]

Australia, Canada, and other countries weighed in with similar sentiments, and when the debacle had come to a close, Len Burman of the *Christian Science Monitor* wrote on December 18, 2011,

> Sometime today, Congress will pass a bill to keep the government funded through September 2012. It will not reflect a careful and balanced assessment of the nation's needs and priorities and how well government programs are meeting those needs. It will reflect the fact that government would shut down at midnight if legislators don't act and the fact that our lawmakers really would like to go home for the holidays. CNN calls 2011 "a year for flirting with government shutdowns" and chronicles a year-long game of chicken played by our policy makers. It should be a wake-up call. This is a really stupid way to make tax-and-spending decisions.[31]

How does all of this behavior compare with that of the framers of the Constitution? Norman Ornstein is happy to answer that question in "Worst. Congress. Ever":

> Partisan and ideological conflict is inherent in democratic political systems, of course, and governing is often a messy process. But this level of dysfunction is not typical ... The Framers saw deliberation, institutional loyalty, and compromise as the only way

---

30 http://arabnews.com/opinion/editorial/article479678.ece.
31 http://www.csmonitor.com/Business/Tax-VOX/2011/1218/Budget-brinkmanship-in-Congress-must-end.

to produce sensible and legitimate policy decisions in an extended republic. Many Republicans, especially former office holders, understand this. Many of the party's current members surely would prefer to solve problems, if the culture and atmosphere—and the primary process that gives inordinate power to both parties' ideological bases—did not make it so hard to do so. But there is little chance that a suitable climate for compromise and bipartisanship will take hold anytime soon—meaning that we can look forward to more headaches at home and abroad.

Taxation and Spending

In August 2011, an op-ed piece in the *New York Times* called "Stop Coddling the Super-Rich" sparked a great deal of commentary with its assertion that the rich needed to be held to the same taxation standards as the poor. This opinion belonged not to a struggling impoverished American, but to Warren Buffett, ranked the third-richest man in the world in 2011. Buffett wrote,

> While the poor and middle class fight for us in Afghanistan, and while most Americans struggle to make ends meet, we mega-rich continue to get our extraordinary tax breaks ... It's nice to have friends in high places ... [The tax] I paid was only 17.4 percent of my taxable income—and that's actually a lower percentage than was paid by any of the other 20 people in our office. Their tax burdens ranged from 33 percent to 41 percent and averaged 36 percent.[32]

In other words, as President Barack Obama later commented in a weekly address, Buffett "is paying a lower rate than his secretary":

> That's not fair. It doesn't make any sense ... Now, some people call this class warfare. But I think asking a billionaire to pay at

[32] http://www.nytimes.com/2011/08/15/opinion/stop-coddling-the-super-rich. html?_r=1.

least the same tax rate as his secretary is just common sense. We don't *envy* success in this country. We *aspire* to it. But we also believe that anyone who does well for themselves should do their fair share in return, so that more people have the opportunity to get ahead—not just a few.[33]

Regardless of whether you consider a proposed *Buffett rule*, which encourages equality in taxation, a good idea, we can pretty safely accept it as fact that the tax code of the United States is quite complicated, full of deductions and loopholes. It seems safe to say that when Warren Buffett can pay a lower percentage than his secretary, some examination of the tax code is in order.

The United States is in trillions of dollars of debt. If the government is willing to forego taxation equality, it's at least willing to be frugal in its expenditures, right?

That depends on whether you think taxpayers should be willing to lose $60.2 million on the production and distribution of pennies in a single year, or whether the relocation of three and a half miles of highway should cost $14.6 billion, just to name two examples out of a countless number of instances of extravagant spending.

According to Jeff Sommer of the *New York Times,* each penny costs 2.4 cents to manufacture. You don't have to be a math whiz to feel concerned that the government is spending 2.4 cents on every solitary cent of currency.

Some worry that abandoning the penny will causes prices to rise, but as Sommer observed, "A number of countries, including Australia, New Zealand, Brazil, Finland, the Netherlands, Norway, Sweden, Switzerland, and Britain, have already dropped their lowest-denominated coins, without dire consequences."[34]

At the very least, Congress might consider cheaper manufacturing processes. In 2008, that's exactly what happened: a bill to switch the

33 http://maddowblog.msnbc.msn.com/_news/2012/04/02/10980218-setting-the-stage-for-a-buffett-rule-showdown.
34 http://www.nytimes.com/2012/04/08/your-money/canada-drops-the-penny-but-will-the-us.html?_r=2&hp.

composition of pennies to color-treated steel was introduced that would save the United States more than $500 million in the next decade. The bill died in committee, just as it had in 2002.

The penny issue is … ahem … small change compared to the Big Dig, one of the most famous pork-barrel projects in United States history. This highway relocation project to create a 3.5-mile tunnel in Massachusetts wound up costing $4 billion per *mile*.

Members of Congress had been trying to strike funding for the project, literally, for decades by the time the government finally moved to stop funding in 2000.

"I lost every time in our attempts to curb the spending on it and have closer oversight of it," John McCain, a Republican senator, told a reporter for the *Boston Globe* in 2006. "When the whole long saga is written in books, it'll astonish people."[35]

Permanent Campaigns

Thanks to intense partisan competition and the need to acquire funds, no given congressman or congresswoman can focus solely on governing America. He or she has the campaign to worry about, after all. In a 2000 article by the American Enterprise Institute, a group of writers opined that:

> We live in the age of the "permanent campaign," when the line between campaigning and governing has blurred, when pollsters are consulted on nearly every matter of policy, and when the old Congressional customs of comity have given way to roll call votes designed solely to frame campaign commercials.[36]

Norman Ornstein wrote in the *Boston Review,*

---

[35] http://www.boston.com/news/local/articles/2006/08/06/big_dig_failures_ threaten_federal_funding/.

[36] http://www.aei.org/article/politics-and-public-opinion/elections/the-permanent- campaign-and-its-future/.

When I arrived in Washington, D.C. there were two distinct seasons—a campaign one, and a governing one. Campaigns understandably used the metaphors of war. Governing, on the other hand, is an additive process, often requiring broad coalitions to craft significant public policy and to sell it to a public worried about short-term change. Norms reinforced this mind-set: lawmakers would never campaign directly against their colleagues from other districts or states, especially not on those colleagues' turf. Campaign consultants and pollsters used to disappear after elections, but now they stick around as consultants, aids, and lobbyists, ever-present.

For a real-life glimpse of how the permanent campaign might disrupt a Congressional office, one needs only to look at the allegations levied against US Representative Tim Murphy in 2006. Staff members in Murphy's office claimed that they had been asked to devote their office time to "labeling, stuffing and mailing greeting cards to individuals who were campaign contributors of Mr. Murphy's," according to the *Pittsburgh Post-Gazette*.[37]

The article also reported that "House ethics rules for members say no campaign activities may take place in any Congressional office."

But as staffer Emily Campbell recalled, "Congressman Murphy would very often say, 'Don't you people care about your jobs? If I'm not reelected, you don't have jobs.'"

In response to such a question, a Congressional employee might ask, "Don't you care about governing the country?"

---

[37] http://www.post-gazette.com/stories/news/politics-federal/Congressman-facing-ethics-flap-456744/.

CHAPTER 5

AMERICA'S FOUNDATION

All Americans, whether they are elected politicians or not, could stand to review the Four Foundations of Freedom. As espoused by the Founding Fathers, the Four Foundations of Freedom are, in order of importance:

- private virtue
- public virtue
- widespread education
- auxiliary precautions

Let's talk about what these mean. *Private virtue* refers to each citizen's responsibility for being a person of integrity. This means, in order for a country that is free to hold itself together, every person—particularly every leader—is mandated to develop and follow his or her own moral compass, which includes following his or her heart and serving his or her family and others in a responsible and compassionate way.

John Adams, a signer of the Declaration of Independence from Massachusetts and the second president of the United States, spoke to the link between the first and second foundation quite succinctly. He said, "Public virtue cannot exist in a nation without private, and public virtue is the only foundation of republics."

Public virtue speaks to the need a democratic republic has for its members to voluntarily sacrifice personal benefit for something greater than themselves. It means leaders and citizens alike must understand they are part of a *society*. That society has needs that are greater than any individual's gain. For example, George Washington ended up serving two terms as president of the United States. Before he accepted that post the first time, he wrote that it "would be the greatest sacrifice of my personal feelings and wishes that ever I have been called upon to make."

Washington realized that a nation often takes on the characteristics of its leaders. Therefore, he was very conscious of the impact his personality had on his electorate. He always tried very hard to be a good role model and to not allow the power of the office to detract from good executive decision making. Because of his love of country and its foundational documents, he tried very hard to live up to the principles contained therein. In that sense, he tried to incorporate his private and public virtues every day in the nation's governance.

Throughout these pages, I have shown how both Republican and Democratic politicians have lacked the private and public virtues necessary for good governance to take place. What is more than a little bit alarming is that these violations of those virtues' foundations have increased in frequency from one year to the next. Unless our governing politicians stem the tide of serving themselves over serving their country's citizens, it will result in our country's government being destroyed, and what results from that will not be to anybody's liking.

The third foundation they identified was *widespread education*. The founders knew that only an educated public could create a strong republic. If a free country determines its fate by the decisions of its citizens, then its politics need to be conducted like a conversation among educated men. Leaders and citizens must understand what each other was talking about; therefore, a liberal (meaning diverse in subject matter), classical education designed to teach people *how* to think—not what to think—needed to be accessible to everyone. This was very much attuned to Thomas Jefferson's thoughts on education: "Educate and inform the whole mass of the people. They are the only sure reliance for the preservation of our liberty."

In view of my intention to remain as nonpartisan and politically neutral as I can, I choose to draw on materials from a variety of sources and viewpoints. One invaluable source on the topic of our country's commitment to education is the conservative thinker John Creech. He is the academic director and a contributing writer for the Republican-leaning blog *The Center for the American Republic,* whose mission is "to form conservative leaders through the study of the history and principles of the American Republic and its roots in Western Civilization."

Writing for that blog, Creech wrote an instructive article entitled "The Classical, Liberal Arts Education of the Founding Fathers." In it, he mentions that the Founding Fathers urged their newly formed country to adopt the kind of education that they were schooled under, which was learning "fluency in both Latin and Greek in order to read core texts in their original languages, texts such as the Greek New Testament, Homer, Cicero, Virgil, and Polybius." The founders felt that by learning classical literature and history, the population would acquire a "shared wisdom," which would further develop and sustain personal and public virtue, both essential to maintain if their new republic would survive the political rigors of time. Therefore, education's main goal was to maintain and preserve their republican form of government.

The bottom line of this kind of education was to not only make one a good person, or follow the tenets contained in *private virtue,* but it also had a public dimension. It was meant to lay the foundation for self-sacrifice and generosity of spirit in service of the republic's "common good," which *public virtue* espouses.

Auxiliary precautions are the various structures and processes created to contain the system of governing they were creating. These included the three coequal branches of government, the system of checks and balances, the electoral college, and so on. These structures provide the parameters for fair debate, balance and distribution of power, compromise, and clean and fair elections.

These functions of government were built into our system to help our leaders avoid the political and self-serving pitfalls that tempt the powerful to sacrifice good governance for expedience and personal gain.

They were meant as precautions, surely, should our leaders' two-fold virtue and the citizenry's critical thinking fail. Such functions would then take over, guiding us down the right path, sustaining the vision of a form of government that protects life, liberty, and the pursuit of happiness. But it's important to note that these structures, which are seemingly the only ones we acknowledge today, were *fourth* in order of importance for providing the foundation of freedom; in fact they were named *auxiliary* functions—supplementary, adjunct, secondary—and were never meant to supplant private and public virtue and widespread education.

When one of the first two virtues are violated (private or public virtue), then the whole political house of cards starts to collapse, and the politician or other office holder has damaged not only his or her integrity, but our nation's integrity as well.

Case in point: the Supreme Court's Citizens United, super-PAC judicial decision. Realizing the auxiliary precautions include the proper and unbiased functioning of the three branches of government, and that each branch must be comprised of members having integrity if the government is going to be able to serve the people in the best possible way, it becomes clear that public integrity failed when our judicial branch upheld Citizens United.

That decision allows political-action committees to raise and spend unlimited amounts of money from corporations, unions, individuals, and associations to advocate for the election or defeat of candidates for federal office by purchasing media advertising like television, radio, and print marketing.

Here's the rub. Corporations, in particular, while being given status as a person in terms of free speech rights, can contribute *millions* of dollars in an effort to support or defeat a political candidate. That's because the contributing entity is *not* treated like an individual contributor, where the limit is $2,500 from individuals per election. It's not unreasonable to assume that the candidate who is able to receive significantly more monetary support from super-PAC advertising will defeat the candidate who has considerably less or no support from the super-PAC contributors.

Where's the integrity in that? Where's the equality?

If this Supreme Court decision is allowed to stand for an extended period of time—or expands to overturn state laws, as it did recently in Montana, then that decision will further amplify the chances that future federal election outcomes will be determined more by how much money is behind a candidate, than the rhetoric or ideas that the candidate espouses. The more time this scandalous event dominates, the more and more irrelevant our auxiliary precautions become—resulting in the endangerment of our whole system of government due to the greater likelihood of clear and significant irregularities in elections. All of which was sanctioned by our Supreme Court.

The founders consistently thought that, in the *absence* of these freedom foundations, no society could survive or at least maintain its liberty. Those assets represented the glue or mortar that provided the Constitution with the underpinnings of what was essential and important to consider when framing it.

It might be that we see these men we call our Founding Fathers as extraordinary simply because they lived by these virtues that they identified as so crucial to maintaining a free country. We might speculate that if these virtues had not been part and parcel of their very souls—and in that way internalized and incorporated into their very being when they fought British oppression during the Revolutionary War—they would never have been willing to sacrifice their property and even their lives to protect their liberties and their nation's integrity.

Certainly, they would not have been able to craft such powerful documents as the Declaration of Independence, the Constitution, and the Bill of Rights, infused as they are with timeless truths, without truly living those internal values. Instead, those documents would be vacuous and meaningless, filled with private agendas, and expedient clauses, and their newly formed republic would ultimately crumble. The weakness, if not utter lack, of these virtues today in how we teach our children and in what we expect out of our citizenry, much less in our elected officials and our business leaders, speaks to the danger we are in of losing our society today.

The upside for societies that cultivate and nurture the Four Foundations of Freedom is they will enjoy prosperity, peace, and happiness in a way that wouldn't be possible if those foundational values were ignored or discounted. It's not enough for the *minority* of Americans to hold the foundations that freedom dictates, but rather, a *majority* of America's citizenry have to passionately and purposely seek those virtues if the benefits of a republican form of democracy will be realized.

As Benjamin Franklin said, "Only a virtuous people are capable of freedom. As nations become corrupt and vicious, they have more need of master."

James Madison added:

> We have staked the whole future of American civilization, not upon the power of government, far from it. We have staked the future of all our political institutions upon the capacity of mankind for self-government upon the capacity of each and all of us to govern ourselves, to control ourselves.

The Founding Fathers' View of Their Constitution

Clearly, it was the framers' willingness to compromise—a direct result of their shared belief in public virtue and its mandate to sacrifice personal desires to the public good—that the Constitution came to pass. It was only through compromise that all their disagreements could be resolved, and because they understood that compromise would always be required, they knew a structure to facilitate the parameters of fair compromise needed to be written.

Washington was an avid supporter of the Constitution. He marveled at how men with such discordant backgrounds, divergent interests, and passionate concerns could all come together as delegates and hammer out a document with such a "spirit of amity and mutual concession." The fact that they were able to unite to form a republic with agreed-upon and well-founded objectives was "little short of a miracle," even according to our first president. They did that because they all were willing to find the middle ground. by putting aside their selfish interests and concerns for something bigger and greater than themselves—all done for the good of the republic.[38]

---

38 Ron Chernow. *Washington*, New York: Penguin Press, 2010, p. 538.

After the Constitutional Convention had adjourned, allegedly, a citizen had asked Benjamin Franklin what kind of government had been structured by the Founding Fathers, to which he replied, "a republic, if you can keep it." He was alluding to the difficulty of sustaining liberty and fairness alike. He knew if future politicians did not respect the Constitution for what it limits and outlines, and provide for representation of every American, and if they were not willing to compromise and pass legislation that attempted to meet the needs of all Americans, then our republic—our democracy—would not survive the test of time.[39]

In order to more clearly understand what Franklin was warning us about, let's look at the differences that exist between the Republican and Democratic parties as they exist today, in the twenty-first century.

The Republican and Democratic Doctrines

If we look at the basic tenets of both the Republican or Democratic parties, we can see they are antithetical to one another and the conclusions they reach as a result of them will remain so unless compromise is achieved. Of course, we must remember that in a democracy we don't need to believe the same things or see the world through the same lenses, but we do have to respect others' points of view, looking for—*and finding*—ways to compromise toward the common good. That's where those virtues come in handy. As long as we don't compromise our integrities at the expense of others, or to satisfy our selfish appetites, and we use empathy and compassion in the process, *and* it's for the common good, then what's under discussion, is worthy of compromise.

The Republican credo is the belief in the need for small government— the less government the better—states' rights, the survival of the fittest. In this view, people should be able to keep what they earn, taxes should

---

39 Ibid. After the Constitutional Convention had adjourned, according to Chernow "Benjamin Franklin shared this view. Legend claims that as he left the State House, Franklin bumped into Elizabeth Powel, who inquired about the form of government produced inside. 'A republic, madam, if you can keep it,' Franklin replied. Powel later claimed that she had no recollection of the famous retort, but she did say that 'the most respectable, influential members of the convention' had gathered at her house and that 'the all-important subject was frequently discussed' there."

be limited, and the Constitution should be interpreted literally, word for word, no more no less.

The Democratic creed is the belief in the importance of adequately caring for all Americans, particularly those who don't have the means or resources to care for themselves—if a larger government is needed to accomplish that goal, so be it—and a graduated system of taxation, whereby, those who are able to pay more taxes should do so, as long as it's fair and equitable. The interpretation of the Constitution should not be *literal,* if by doing so, it doesn't reflect the changing times and needs of its citizenry.

Of course, there are other differences, but here I want to illustrate the opposing parameters through which each political camp views the role of government in the lives of all Americans.

Interestingly, these opposing views were the same ones our Founding Fathers held during the writing of the Constitution. Yet they were able to come up with a document that safeguarded the rights of all Americans. They took aim at what would be necessary to protect our republic from destruction by human frailty.

They also knew that the Four Foundations of Freedom would have to be respected if our republic would survive. They believed in order to mirror their intent in writing the Constitution, the political representatives who represent us would need to be willing to compromise so that legislation got passed and all Americans could participate in the benefits that come from being part of this great country. After all, these powerful documents, the sacred texts of a secular society of free citizens, were written for all the people who would have the privilege and honor to be American citizens.

The founders gave their nation's future generations the obligation to ask themselves some strong questions: Are we honoring our sacred documents? Do we still see ourselves in the words "We the People"? Do our leaders and our laws hold to the crucial Four Foundations of Freedom? Or does our behavior risk our republic?

In the next chapter, we will discuss the principal factors that influence today's politicians. Are they shirking their duty to do what's best for our country?

CHAPTER 6

POLITICS AND INTEGRITY

I t might seem that putting the words *politics* and *integrity* together on the same page is an oxymoron. Those two concepts are like oil and water to some—they don't mix! Aren't they contradictory terms, like the expression *deafening silence?*

In this chapter I explain why in today's world, politics and integrity don't seem to blend and suggest how we can fix it so that those two seemingly contradictory concepts can work side by side in perfect unison to further our nation's goals.

Ironically, the word *politics* actually means *a conversation between citizens.* In that definition, it would be assumed that these citizens would sit at a common table of mutual respect and integrity. If that were the case, these concepts wouldn't be as antithetical as they seem to be in the political world today. But today, no one seems to respect one another's senses of integrity. If we could only change the conversants' table to glass rather than solid and opaque—then each other's integrity, not to mention what's up their sleeves, would be more transparent!

But working definitions of politics and integrity are in order. Interestingly, the definitions of *politician* offered by *Webster's New Universal Unabridged Dictionary* is not particularly flattering. Some definitions in the entry, like "a person who is active in party politics" and "a person who

61

holds political office," are fairly straightforward. But other definitions, which include "a seeker or holder of public office, who is more concerned about winning favor or retaining power than maintaining principles," and "a person who seeks to gain power ... in ways that are generally disapproved," speak of the distasteful culture surrounding politics today.

"*Politician* is more often derogatory," the entry explains. "*Politician* suggests the schemes and devices of a person who engages in (esp. small) politics for party ends or for one's own advantage: *a dishonest politician.*"

Webster notes that *statesman,* on the other hand, "suggests the eminent ability, foresight, and unselfish patriotic devotion of a person dealing with (esp. important or great) affairs of state: *a distinguished statesman.*"

Quite clearly, many of our Founding Fathers were excellent examples of statesmen. That's because they tried to embrace and follow the tenets as espoused in their Four Foundations of Freedom, particularly the first two and, arguably, the most important codes of belief: private and public virtues (see chapter 5).

Private virtue simply means being a person of integrity and public virtue means being willing to sacrifice personal interest or gain for the good of society. Since private virtue means being ethically and morally consistent and truthful, a good working definition of what integrity is would be what is written on the walls of one of the United States Air Force Academy rooms: "Integrity is doing the right thing when no one's looking."

But integrity means more than that. It refers to being "whole and undivided," or being *unwilling* to sacrifice one's principles for short-term gain and profit. However, there may be instances where we must be more flexible and less rigid, even willing to sacrifice some of our integrity for a long-term gain for the common good, as President Lincoln did when he wrote to Horace Greely, a prominent American newspaper editor, on August 22, 1862. Lincoln wrote, "If I could save the Union without freeing any slave I would do it, and if I could save it by freeing all the slaves, I would do it; and if I could save it by freeing some and leaving others alone, I would also do that. What I do about slavery, and the colored race, I do because I believe it helps to save the Union; and what I forbear, I forbear because I do not believe it would help to save the Union."[40]

Clearly, integrity is a more fluid thing than even the best of us let on. Because of the human condition and the fact that none of us is perfect, from time to time we are all subject to seeking short-term rewards at the expense of long-term gains and satisfactions. To the degree that such rewards *violate* our principles and beliefs and *damage* our integrity, such thinking and behavior ultimately has a negative effect upon others.

We expect our elected officials to maintain private virtue, but, since they are elected to serve *the people,* they also must develop public virtue. Unfortunately, many of our elected officials are politicians in the worst sense of the word—they lack the public virtue of statesmen.

This chapter will explain why that is so.

Statesmen and Stateswomen

As part of our working definition of what our leaders *should* be, let us speak of statesmen and stateswomen, those elected officials who, whether on a local or national level, are *other*-centered. They should have a strong drive to be of service to others. It must be a motive above and beyond many other possible drives pressing for expression. Just helping others should be an end in itself. And they should feel it's a real privilege and honor to be of service to others and their country. Or to put it simply, they should exhibit private and public virtue. We expect no less from our firefighters and social workers; let us expect of it of our politicians too.

In the case of private virtue, they should be persons of integrity: honest, transparent, and trustworthy. In the case of public virtue, they must also possess the qualities of being other-centered and willing to sacrifice personal benefit or selfish wishes and desires for more altruistic concerns, such as responding to the needs of *all* Americans, regardless of party affiliation, race, or ethnicity.

---

[40] Abraham Lincoln Online, Speeches and Writing, "Letter to Horace Greeley," http://showcase.netins.net/web/creative/lincoln/speeches/greeley.htm.

Examples of Public Virtue

Some of the Founding Fathers demonstrated their commitment to public virtue by sacrificing time with their families when they were writing the Declaration of Independence. They did this because they were willing to be part of a movement, idea, or a belief that was greater than themselves, putting their country first, before their own personal interests. Benjamin Franklin missed his daughter's wedding and, to his great sorrow, the death and funeral of his wife because of his commitments internationally. Abigail Adams gave birth to a stillborn daughter while her husband was away in Philadelphia. Thomas Jefferson lost a two-year-old daughter to whooping cough. It took seven months for word to reach him in France.

At the birth of our nation, the term *public virtue* meant to voluntarily sacrifice personal benefit or interest for the good of society. How many more than a handful of today's politicians have our country's best interests at heart when they swear to protect the Constitution? There's no question we need more men and women in public service willing to look beyond their own selfish interests and the next election and toward what's best for the next generation and beyond. We need people serving because of love of country, who want to make a positive difference and *not* because they want to advance themselves ahead of the people they serve. We need people who are willing to take a stand and tell the truth, even if it is politically unpopular. In short, we need statesmen and stateswomen who know that securing the blessings of liberty is worth any cost, providing, of course, the price in human lives and treasure *is* worth it, and the country's objective is consonant with the long-term safety and protection of its citizenry.

Let us compare and contrast what today's politicians may view as "feeling like a winner" with how our Founding Fathers perceived the measurement of success.

Measures of Success—Then and Now

Since what success means to each of us is such a personal question, I would imagine it has different meaning for every one of us, depending on our life circumstances. What I may view as successful may be different from what you see success to be, and vice versa.

However, for many people, the *gold standard* of success is how wealthy we are. The wealthier we are, the more successful we may feel we are, and the more successful others may perceive us to be as well. I have no statistics to support that statement, but just observing comments made by others and how they conduct their lives, making money and lots of it, seems very important to many people in our culture.

We can also use the attainment of *status* as another measurement of success, regardless if it's earned or given as a birthright. If that's the parameter used, it isn't any different today than it was in the 1700s. That's because the societal values have remained constant down through the ages, meaning societal status was as important during the Founding Fathers' time as it appears to be today: the wealthier you were then or now, the higher the class you were perceived by others to be in. So, in that sense, during our forefathers' time, the measure of success was perhaps the same as it is now. That's because the status of the wealthy was every bit in place then, as it is now, and nearly all those who remained involved in politics after the war were wealthy, the poorer patriots having been run out of the inner circles.

Saying that, since status was already attained and more pressing matters were at hand during the time leading up to the Revolutionary War and immediately afterward, we might speculate that status itself diminished in importance from what it might have been when America was still a colony, as well as the self-centered agenda that status seeking requires.

They had a country to build, after all, and if that failed, status would be the least of their worries. For that reason, they had to be *other*-centered and not concerned with their stations in life at the time they wrote those marvelous documents and set up the structure of our government. The spirit of cooperation that they showed each other at that time was proof in itself that they were eager to do something above and beyond satisfying their own narcissistic and selfish needs, and in so doing, provide the road map, as contained in those documents, so necessary if freedom was to survive for future generations to enjoy.

Many of the Founding Fathers were very wealthy. According to the history included on the website of a US embassy abroad, "Except for slaves, standards of living were generally high—higher, in fact, than in England itself. Because English investors had withdrawn, the field was open to entrepreneurs among the colonists."[41] The fact that the Founding Fathers and their countrymen, were willing to risk all, including their lives, for the greater good, speaks to their priorities of favoring their liberties over financial or material success.

I can only imagine the sense of pride that they and their fellow countrymen must have felt when they acted as a community and did something that was greater than themselves, and in so doing, knew that what they were doing was not only for them, but for future generations as well. The gift that was given included a *theory* of self-governance (the Declaration of Independence), a *formula* (the Four Foundations of Freedom), and the means to carry them out (the Constitution and the Bill of Rights). They did that not for personal gain and adulation, but rather, for the good of their newly born country and for the generations of citizens who would have the opportunity to be a part of this great nation in the future.

The kinds of feelings the founders must have felt when they gathered to write those various documents, where they all were working for something greater than themselves, must have been the kinds of feelings I felt when, during the truce, I served in Korea.

What my Korean experience gave me was a sense of pride that I had the opportunity to serve my country. I feel so thankful that I am an American. I realize that my being born in America was happenstance, but also know that didn't diminish its value or appreciation for me. Because my parents gave me so much, as well as did so many others who I met in my sojourn through life, I felt I had to give back to society what they had given me.

However, I realize I'll never be able to give back what I received from simply being an American. The greatest thing that anyone who has touched my life has given me was their love. And that is exactly what the people who came before us have given all of us as well. That was demonstrated by their fighting for our freedoms, for their *caring for* others besides themselves,

---

41 Christopher Conte, United States Diplomatic Mission to Germany, "The US Economy: A Brief History" http://usa.usembassy.de/etexts/oecon/chap3.htm. (15 Jul. 2012).

and for the *love* they felt for one another, their nation, and their future generations. Because if it wasn't for the Declaration of Independence, the Constitution, and the Bill of Rights, those of us who have been able to profit from those documents would never be as proud to be Americans as we once were, but don't feel today.

I don't believe the citizens or the politicians of today, including myself at one time, mirror our Founding Fathers' attitudes and feelings for each other or their country, or appreciate the part love plays in how we, as Americans, view ourselves or our country today.

Tom Kertscher, writing an article for the website politifact.com, wrote an article entitled *Political Vitriol Is Bad These Days, but Experts Say It's Been Worse,* in which he quotes University of Wisconsin-Whitewater communication professor Richard Haven. "The instant communication—and the increased tendency of politicians to take extreme positions and demonize their opponents—have put political civility at its lowest ebb in the past 25 years."

Well, it was never exactly pie in the sky. In earlier centuries, Alexander Hamilton shot and killed his political rival! People used to draw and quarter each other for minor infractions (that's dismemberment behind four horses), lynch African Americans (that's hang and mutilate), imprison Chinese and Japanese immigrants in work camps. Our forefathers *owned people,* enslaving those whose work built their fortunes, and disclaimed the children they fathered with slave women not free to refuse them in bed. So we've always had lots of problems living up to our documented ideals.

Political incivility prior to our twenty-first century was, in many cases, more horrendous in terms of crimes against humanity compared to the kinds of calculated infractions that our politicians have inflicted upon each other and their fellow Americans today. But that doesn't make it right! It is crucial that we continue holding our feet and hands to the fire: perhaps one day we will get there.

Whenever self-aggrandizement occurs in the political arena, what gets damaged even further is the public's perception of the political process. Congress can hardly have its public-approval rating be much lower than it already is, which is at 10 percent, for if it gets much lower, it will fall in the minus category. Then there are a number of voters who will stick with the party and vote the straight party line, no matter what! If that kind of political irresponsibility reigns supreme for an inordinate amount of time, the end result is the respect for the democratic process will become further bruised and battered.

Eventually, our system of government—as we know it—will become null and void, because people will have lost faith in their political institutions being able to care for their needs in a responsible and meaningful way, and possibly seek other ways less-than-lawful to get their needs met.

For example, the "99 percenters" demonstrating throughout the country as part of the Occupy movement, which supports *everyman causes* such as affordable housing and health care, have generally been peaceful with small pockets of unlawful behavior; however, if their unrest grows, due to a growing number of people feeling that government is not doing enough to rectify the problems of the majority, as time passes, more violent demonstrations may result.

Another accompanying problem that exacerbates and encourages demonstrations against our government over the years is that our elected officials, our politicians, have never fully appreciated the part formal education can play in helping preserve and safeguard our republic, our freedoms, and our democracy.

Returning to John Creech's article, "The Classical, Liberal Arts Education of the Founding Fathers," appearing on the Center for the American Republic website, he mentions that the Founding Fathers urged their newly formed country to adopt the kind of education whose main goal was to maintain and preserve their republican form of government. Creech points out that "education today is mostly aimed at the hope of securing lucrative employment." Though education focusing on our nation's economic well-being is important, that alone will not save our republic from eventual downfall.

That's because, first of all, I believe, using the acquisition of material property alone—or dollars earned—as a measure of an individual's success is a poor barometer of a person's overall self-worth. What I believe is ignored in our twenty-first-century educational system is the part that the concepts of private and public virtue play in American's thinking today. It's nonexistent. Our Founding Fathers have clearly stated that unless those two virtues are incorporated into our school systems' curricula, and therefore into each of our citizen's thinking, and, specifically, most certainly the thinking of our politicians, our civil servants—our republic and democracy as we know it today will ultimately fail. Samuel Adams thought it was so important that he put it this way, "Public virtue cannot exist in a nation without private, and public virtue is the only foundation of republics."[42]

Democracy is the means whereby our economic system, or the private ownership of capital, namely, capitalism, can thrive—at least that is how it is supposed to work in theory. However, in today's world, that conventional wisdom is starting to go down the tubes. According to *Newsweek's* "Best Opinion: *Daily Beast, Reuters,* and *Time* Magazine" the week of March 28, 2012, all agree, "China is winning the future":

"China is smoking us," says Zachary Karabell at *The Daily Beast.* Both the U.S. and China engage in a lot of government spending, but China puts its money into infrastructure, transportation, alternate energy, and housing, all of which "will yield long-term benefits for the Chinese economy." The U.S., on the other hand, spends on "consumption, safety nets, and the military," which comprise a shakier foundation for economic growth. The "sclerotic inability" of the U.S. government to "productively invest for the common future" is the reason why its "form of capitalism has ceased to fulfill hopes, dreams, and needs of far too many people.

For in our democratic society, the Constitution guarantees all Americans "life, liberty and the pursuit of happiness." In those freedoms, is the freedom of opportunity, which in the case of capitalism, is to pursue

---

[42] John Adams to Mercy Warren, 16 Apr. 1776, in Philip B. Kurland and Ralph Lerner, "Epilogue: Securing the Republic," *The Founders Constitution,* http://press-pubs.uchicago.edu/founders/documents/v1ch18s9.html.

your economic dreams of success, as long as the freedom to pursue those dreams are lawful. Such laws are contained in our Constitution. However, we must not confuse the economic system of capitalism with liberty. Freedom of opportunity is what is protected by the Constitution, but *capitalism,* per se, is not. Capitalism only refers to the private ownership of capital—money. Sadly, but still true, it costs so much for a sole proprietor to compete with the big boys that most of us are just corporate serfs in today's economy. Where's the democracy in that?

The end goal for all capitalistic endeavors is to make money. Successful competition is the driving force that determines the success of any capitalistic endeavor. Shouldn't our economic system also require public and private virtue? What about that? Just as we limit and regulate democracy so the republic can protect the common good, preventing the tyranny of the majority from overpowering the minority, government has a role to play in limiting and regulating *capitalist* practices, *so the republic protects the common good* by preventing the tyranny of the wealthy few from overpowering everyone else.

Democracy can serve the corporate world by providing the mechanisms in which businesses satisfactorily compete with other businesses to provide the goods and services that the public desires, and it also serves the American citizen by providing the legislation for our government to satisfactorily respond to the needs of the public. After all, that's who democracy was originally intended to serve—the people—not exclusively corporations.

We must remember that our Constitution *replaced* the Articles of Confederation, and in order for our Constitution to serve our republic the best, a democratic form of government was formed, where "all people living in America would have fair representation" and, in that way, a level playing field so that they would have an equal *opportunity* to pursue their dreams regardless of who they were, as long as they did so in a "law-abiding way." The truth is that *all* the people would not have fair representation for almost two centuries, as the right to vote was granted to women and all people of color only gradually, and still not practiced fairly or equally in every state for every legal citizen until the Voting Rights Act of 1970.

Unfortunately, over time, our politicians, who represent each of us, have moved further and further away from cooperation with one another for the greater good and serving the American people the way our democracy intended them to do. In its place, the corporate model of competition has taken over between and among politicians; this works for the benefit of the politician at the expense of the voting taxpayer whom he or she is expected to serve. What is necessary is to replace corporate power with people power. Corporate power, or the winner-take-all mentality, may work for the politician, but it doesn't work for the people because no compromise can be achieved.

It's a curious paradox that while politicians do seem to compromise and cooperate less than before, the way they did so before left out huge portions of the population: women, working people, and people of color. So was that cooperation in good spirit for the good of all, or was it a closed boys' club that kept resources and wealth to a few? That's what's happening now too; it's just more blatant because the victims of it are 99 percent of us, not just those *designated* to be disaffected. This might be ultimately good for the republic—if "We the People" can get over our divisions.

With people power, instead of each politician *competing* with each other for the people's votes, we replace that corporate model of competition, with the democratic model of a spirit of *cooperation* between the two parties, they will then have the same goal in mind: to practice good government by serving the needs of *all* of America's base, not just their party's or the special-interest groups that vie for unique considerations and governmental contracts. When the democratic process as envisioned by our forefathers is working optimally, who benefits? We all do, and as a result, America is all the better for it because we are once again following the dictates as stated by our forefathers.

Washington Represented the Ideal Politician

Now, I know what you're thinking, that here, in the twenty-first century, that's just *not* what's happening. And my response is, yes, that's true. I'm talking about the *ideal standard* that all politicians should strive to approach, much like what our Founding Fathers perceived their mission to be when they signed the Declaration of Independence.

71

Contrary to the way things are today, Washington was an example of a public servant, or politician, par excellence. If young people wish to choose politics as a field to pursue, modeling their political aspirations after one of the greatest presidents of all time wouldn't be a bad thing to do.

Empathy and Compassion

Empathy is being able to put ourselves in another's shoes, or even to see a little bit of ourselves in other people. It is the ability to feel what someone else feels whether we have ever been in their shoes or not. Compassion is being able to care *about* what another is going through, to feel *for* them; empathy is being able to feel it. When we're able to do that, we're able to understand what that person needs. It is through empathy and compassion, that we're able to develop a much greater appreciation of what others are experiencing, which also provides us with a richer life experience for ourselves as well.

Imbedded in the public and private virtues, is the quality of *empathy.* Being honest and moral and other-centered requires one to look through other people's eyes to know *how* to serve them, and in so doing, see a little bit of oneself in whomever one is relating to. That is why I believe all politicians need to be empathetic and compassionate to the needs of their electorate. By being empathetic and compassionate, politicians express their own humanness or goodness toward their voters, and in that way show their public and private virtue in loving and caring ways. When they've succeeded, politicians can reflect what's in their hearts and souls. On a national level, that is part of all that's good about being an American.

According to his biographer, Ron Chernow, Washington showed his compassionate and *enlightened spirit* when "he generalized the American Revolution into a movement blazing a path toward the universal triumph of freedom."[43] In support of his thesis, Chernow quotes Washington as writing,

> I rejoice in a belief that intellectual light will spring up in the
> dark corners of the earth; that freedom of inquiry will produce

---

[43] Chernow, *Washington*, p. 565.

liberality of conduct; that mankind will reverse the absurd position that *the many* were made for the *few;* and that they will not continue slaves in one part of the globe, when they can become freemen in another. [Chernow's italics][44]

Though, among the delegates, there was great sentiment that slavery should be abolished when the Constitution was written, our forefathers, nevertheless, feared that by outlawing slavery at that time, some of the strongly pro-slave states, of the original thirteen, would bolt the union.

Paradoxically, these pro-slave states also wanted to count the entire Africa-descended population for their census—and representation—figures. A shocking compromise was reached granting *three-quarters personhood* to the slaves. Not enough to count as individual citizens, but enough collectively to swell the ranks of representatives to those states. In this example, the Union was preserved over individual rights *for the benefit of the states claiming to care more about individual rights.* Yes, *quite* an interesting paradox.

Because of the way politics is played today, it is no longer an honorable profession. That's because politicians don't treat with respect the part that private and public virtue, empathy, and compassion play in any political discourse. That is not only true toward the electorate, but also toward many of their fellow politicians.

Such an evil compromise over slavery raises the question of whether there ever was a time when politics wasn't bloodstained. Surely in that case, as now, the "states' rights" contingent was exploiting the "public welfare" contingent for their own gain. Those states were willing to break the union over slavery then, knowing their opponents were not; then they did it again around eighty years later, causing the Civil War; and they continue to hold the Union hostage today—over both individual rights (for women and gay people anyway) as well as public welfare (health care, education, economic justice).

---

44 Ibid, p. 565.

That being the case—that currently politics and integrity don't seem to mix—it *doesn't* mean we shouldn't try to accommodate them into some kind of a meaningful whole. In fact, politics and integrity are inseparable. After all, politicians try to appeal to *voters'* basic values and belief systems so we will embrace their perspective of how we, the voters, should be governed. And when we talk about *your* basic values and beliefs, we're talking about your *integrity*—the most valued and treasured part of your personality.

Some Further Comments on Integrity

Our country doesn't have to look new and shiny as it might have been perceived when this country was founded, shortly after the Declaration of Independence was written and we started calling our country the "United States of America." If our nation still had its integrity intact, it would still look as beautiful as it did at the time of its birth.

I have a plaque and a picture hanging in my office that reminds me of what America means to me and why I'm still proud to be an American. After I wrote the book *The Impotent Giant: How to Reclaim the Moral High Ground of American Politics,* a dear friend gave me a plaque that reminded me what's important in the world of politics today. It reads:

"Integrity, be the change you wish to see in the world."

The picture was a photograph I picked up in New England. It is a picture of an old, tired-looking chair, next to a tired-looking table that sits by a tired-looking window that is in need of paint but has bright and clean white chiffon curtains, overlooking a yard. The picture is a perfect example of what integrity is all about: the desk, table, and window frame were complete and unaltered, and the curtains were clean and fresh. The first thing that came to mind when I viewed the picture was that because everything appeared intact, authentic, and uncompromised, I must treat the picture I was viewing with respect and reverence. I saw beauty and serenity in its worn and aged appearance. That in itself demonstrated the enduring and lasting quality that integrity provides each of our lives.

The only thing we need to do is recognize, hold in highest regard, and nurture our own personal integrity, and if we live with our integrity in mind, we will do what we were put on this earth to do, which is to care for those who could use a helping hand.

What is interesting to me is that when I called the art gallery to purchase the picture, I told the owner that I was going to call it *Integrity,* to which he replied that he had submitted it to an art exhibit and named it *Integrity* as well.

One might well ask, how can I draw a parallel between having a sense of integrity, like the items in the room that seemed to be *intact* and *uncompromised,* and compare that picture to a government that is anything but static, that is, rather, constantly being altered and ever changing, what with new bills being legislated and Congress and presidents ever changing? What should remain constant and unyielding in government is the politicians' integrity—just like in the photograph, where the picture's inherent beauty and charm, its integrity, remains the same regardless of its age. For in both cases, whether we're talking about the items in the photograph or politicians, their integrity must remain uncompromised and authentic over time.

Your integrity is part of your soul. It's the part of your personality that is whole and undivided. It is what you value and what you believe in. If you're living life with integrity, you're living it with honesty, being truthful not only with yourself but with others as well. It's what makes life all worth living. For if you don't have integrity, you have nothing.

You know whether you have jeopardized your sense of integrity by whether or not you have intentionally attacked another's self-esteem or personal worth.

Here, in the twenty-first century, when we look at the lives of our fellow Americans, regardless of the line of work they're in, *dishonesty and unprincipled practices* run rampant in many of our lives. The news media and Internet is fraught with daily examples of people empowered by virtue of their age, gender, employment, or status, who abuse that power and, in so doing, damage their own integrity. A good example are political talk show hosts who regularly demonize the opposition party by labeling the caller or using sound bites and buzz words that exaggerate and make undesirable the differences between the parties of the radio host and the caller, clearly implying that that the *whole* party displays that exaggerated and undesirable characteristic.

I talk in some detail about the power of labels in my earlier book, *The Impotent Giant*. Name-calling is certainly one of the tactics talk show hosts use to demonize their callers' reputations and anyone who might be associated with them, either by party affiliation, sexual orientation, or a host of other markers that make them separate and distinct in an undesirable way from the implied *positive* reputation the radio host claims.

Because empowerment means you are authorized to act and behave in a certain way doesn't mean you can do so irresponsibly. We can excuse people who make *honest* mistakes, because they do so unwittingly, and therefore, don't intentionally damage their or another's sense of integrity. On the other hand, people who deliberately and knowingly engage in self-aggrandizement at the individual, corporate, or governmental levels are guilty of not just a trivial impropriety, but something much greater than that. For being dishonest and unprincipled in their empowered position, they have damaged their integrity. For many, integrity is so important and such a valued part of their personalities that they are willing to fight wars and risk their lives in their effort to protect their country's integrity.

That was certainly true for those who fought in the Revolutionary War, or any of the great wars that this country has been part of, including the wars in Iraq and Afghanistan.

The way you can determine what your integrity is all about is to reflect on your life and decide what's important enough to you that you would be willing to risk your life to protect or defend it.

The word *integrity* no longer comes to mind when we think about what we love about America today. We can occasionally find the rare example of a politician acting in the nation's best interest. For example, Representative Howard Coble of North Carolina "has sponsored bill after bill for the last twenty-eight years to rein in Congressional pensions. He's even opted out of the pension plan. Rep. Coble said taxpayers already pay his salary, and he doesn't believe they should be responsible for a lavish pension."[45] Coble's example is inspiring, but it's considerably less inspiring that he still hasn't succeeded in his efforts—even after three decades.

An example of moral decay at the highest governmental level is the Lewinsky scandal, which was a political scandal that came to the public's attention in 1998. According to Wikipedia, the online encyclopedia, the scandal involved a sexual relationship between then president of the United States William Clinton and a twenty-two-year-old White House intern, Monica Lewinsky.

As the news spread of this extramarital affair, the formation of a grand jury was formed to look into the matter. Ultimately, this led to the US House of Representatives impeaching President Clinton in 1998. The Senate conducted a twenty-one day impeachment trial. Subsequently, President Clinton was acquitted in the Senate on all impeachment charges of perjury and obstruction of justice, and for lying under oath.

During President Clinton's grand jury testimony, the president's response when he was questioned about the truthfulness of his statement that "there is not a sexual relationship, an improper sexual relationship, or any other kind of improper relationship," was carefully worded as he argued, "It depends on what the meaning of the word 'is' is."[46] Obviously he was mincing words and using intellectualization and denial to defend against acknowledging that his encounter with Lewinsky was improper, because it was indeed a sexual liaison.

Lewinsky alleged that, between November 1995 and March 1997, she had nine sexual encounters with President Clinton that, according to her testimony, various sexual acts were performed in the Oval Office, but none of them involved sexual intercourse.

Although Clinton remained in office, he was subsequently cited for contempt of court; he agreed to a five-year suspension of his Arkansas law

---

45 Chris Cuomo. ABC News, 04 Nov. 2011, http://abcnews.go.com/US/chris-cuomos-give-break-Congressional-perks/story?id=14884393#.T4I_-ppAZsw.

46 Wikipedia, "Monica Lewinsky," http://en.wikipedia.org/wiki/Monica_Lewinsky (27 Feb. 2012).

license, starting in 1998. On October 1, 2001, Bill Clinton was barred from practicing law before the Supreme Court of the United States.

Following close on the heels of the Lewinsky scandal, in August 2008, John Edwards, a former United States senator from North Carolina and a Democratic Party presidential candidate admitted to an extramarital affair. It too spiraled into a political scandal. Edwards went on trial on April 23, 2012, accused of using nearly a million dollars in campaign funds to hide the affair. He was acquitted, at the time of this writing, of one count, and the jury hung on all the others, leading to a mistrial that prosecutors say they won't retry.

In place of love of country and its values and ideals, we may feel shame and disgust that there's so much dishonesty in our government, even at the highest levels, so much so that we don't know who to trust and believe in, which in itself makes it difficult to identify with our country.

This unfortunate happening didn't occur overnight. It took many years in the making before we became so egocentric and narcissistic in living our own lives that our primary and only concern is ourselves and our immediate families.

CHAPTER 7

WHEN DID OUR COUNTRY BEGIN GOING DOWN THE WRONG SET OF TRACKS?

S o, how did we as a country lose our way; where—how and when—did our moral compass fail to point true north and cause our country to veer off the proverbial tracks that were supported by our Declaration of Independence, Constitution, and Bill of Rights? What caused those tracks to become so corroded and rusted out—disuse and lack of upkeep? It all began when we entered the Vietnam War, which was in March 1965. Ever since then, the politicians have chosen to ride the *wrong* set of "American" tracks.

That was done because the politicians did not listen to many protests our young men of draft age made, who didn't wish to serve in Vietnam. Protesters expressed their anger and dissatisfaction with our government's policy by burning the American flag in demonstrations against the Vietnam War. Instead of Congress hearing what the protesters were expressing by using their integrity, empathy-hence-compassion, and acting accordingly, Congress passed a law called the federal Flag Protection Act, prohibiting burning the flag.

The law was overturned by the United States Supreme Court as a violation of our First Amendment right of free speech, and Congress quickly passed a new Flag Protection Act, which also was struck down by the Supreme Court. However, Congress was not to be deterred, so, in 1989, they tried to enact flag protection statutes in the form of a constitutional amendment. It didn't pass. Allegedly, each Congress since 1989 has considered creating a flag-desecration amendment.

Jennifer Rosenberg, writing for the website About.com, discusses why the United States involved us in the Vietnamese civil war in the first place.[47] But before I answer that question, we must have a *compassionate* understanding of what the Vietnam people had to struggle with for decades. Just like how we treated our flag burners who protested the Vietnam war.

First, it was the French who interfered with Vietnam's autonomy. The Vietnamese had "suffered under French colonial rule for nearly six decades," writes Rosenberg. Then, during WWII, in 1940, Japan invaded parts of Vietnam. By 1941, Vietnam had French *and* Japanese powers occupying the country. At the same time, Ho Chi Minh, the Communist Vietnamese revolutionary leader returned to Vietnam, after a thirty-year absence traveling the world and studying democracies.

Immediately, Ho established the Viet Minh, an organization that led the effort to remove the French occupiers. Ultimately, Ho gained support from the northern portion of Vietnam, and as Rosenberg writes, the "Viet Minh announced the establishment of an independent Vietnam with a new government called the Democratic Republic of Vietnam on September 2, 1945." The French were unwilling to give up their colony without a fight, so they fought back.

"For years," writes Rosenberg, "Ho had tried to court the United States to support him against the French, including supplying the US with military intelligence about the Japanese during World War II." But that was to no avail. The US was very fearful of Communism spreading throughout the world, and using the *domino theory* as its rationale, held that if one country fell to Communism, other nearby countries would soon

47 Jennifer Rosenberg, "Vietnam War," About.com 2012. http://history1900s.about.com/od/vietnamwar/a/vietnamwar.htm (05 Mar. 2012).

fall as well. It was for that reason that the United States turned its back on Ho's efforts to elicit support for independence and, instead, chose to help the colonizing French defeat Ho and his followers by providing military aid to France in 1950.

After the French left, the United States picked up where they left off, eventually sending military advisers to Vietnam. As time went by, months turned into years, and we committed not only more and more of our advisers to South Vietnam, but eventually our military as well. All done in our stated effort to stop the spread of Communism in that part of the world. It only ended when we pulled our troops out of Vietnam in 1973, having finally come to the conclusion that our military objective of defeating the Communist army of the Viet Cong was not going to happen.

But I'm getting ahead of my story.

According to Rosenberg, after the French were soundly defeated at Dien Bien Phu, in 1954, they decide to pull out of Vietnam. In order to facilitate their peaceful withdrawal from Vietnam in 1954, the Geneva Accords were written, establishing the "temporary division of Vietnam along the seventeenth parallel (which split the country into communist North Vietnam and non-communist South Vietnam)." In 1956, a general democratic election was scheduled to "unite the country under one government," she says. Because the United States feared the Communists would win the election, they refused to endorse the process.

In response to a US request, the country south of the seventeenth parallel—what was soon to be known as South Vietnam—agreed to cooperate with the United States' wishes and held their own elections, involving only the area south of the line of demarcation. "After eliminating most of his rivals, Ngo Dinh Diem was elected. His leadership, however, proved so horrible that he was killed in a 1963 coup that was supported by the United States."

Rosenberg continues to report, "Since Diem had alienated many South Vietnamese during his tenure, Communist sympathizers in South Vietnam established the National Liberation Front (NLF), also known as the Viet Cong."

What prompted the US military forces to involve themselves in the Vietnam conflict was what has come to be known as the Gulf of Tonkin Incident, when North Vietnamese troops fired directly upon two US ships in international waters on the second and fourth of August, 1964. Congress responded by adopting the Gulf of Tonkin Resolution, giving President Lyndon B. Johnson the authority to send troops into Vietnam. Now, instead of only having military *advisors* in Vietnam, we put US boots on the ground as well in March of the next year.

Because President Johnson was only interested in confining the fighting to South Vietnam, and in that way limiting the war only to that area of the country, many interpreted that action as meaning he was no longer interested in winning the war, but only to support and strengthen South Vietnam's defenses until South Vietnam could take over.

Rosenberg agrees, suggesting, "Johnson set the stage for future public and troop disappointment when the US found themselves in a stalemate with the North Vietnamese and the Viet Cong." According to Rosenberg, "By limiting the fighting parameters, the US forces would not conduct a serious ground assault into the North to attack the Communists directly, nor would there be any strong effort to disrupt the Ho Chi Minh Trail (the Viet Cong's supply path that ran through Laos and Cambodia)."

According to Rosenberg, the Viet Cong's Tet Offensive of January 30, 1968, which was a *surprise attack* on about a hundred South Vietnamese cities and towns, proved to American forces that the "enemy was stronger and better organized than they had been led to believe. The Tet Offensive was a turning point in the war, because LBJ, faced now with an unhappy American public and bad news from his military leaders in Vietnam, decided to no longer escalate the war."

This limiting the fighting to contain the enemy rather than fight to win was anathema to many Americans, because winning any conflict had been a cardinal principle whether at a sports event or on the battlefield. It was only in the Korean War, which also resulted in dividing a once singular Korea into North and South, did the American spirit to "play to win" not apply. I believe the Johnson administration was hoping against hope that we could establish a North Vietnam and South Vietnam as we had in Korea. Ultimately, that was not to be, and the Viet Cong eventually won the war and the country.

A ceasefire agreement was finally attained, and the last US troops left Vietnam on March 29, 1973. After all the bloodshed and deaths that had occurred since America's involvement in the Vietnam conflict, from March 1965 and ending in March 1973, eight years later, at least 58,000 Americans died in their effort to keep Communism from spreading in Southeast Asia. And what has happened as a result of all of this effort? Answer: "On July 2, 1976, Vietnam was reunited as a Communist country, the Socialist Republic of Vietnam," concludes Jennifer Rosenberg.

What I was most interested in understanding was why we entered the war in the first place, and did we accomplish the objectives we had for doing so? We know from Rosenberg's excellent article that we entered the Vietnam War to prevent the spread of Communism in Southeast Asia. Because of the nature of the war and the restrictions our government placed on what our military could do to *win* the war, what soon became apparent, was, at *best* we ended up trying to keep South Vietnam from becoming communistic. According to Rosenberg, what we had done was to engage "in a war that many viewed as having no way to win." Rosenberg stated that eventually, our Washington politicians "lost the American public's support for the war." And when that happened, the war was lost. Since the end of the war, Rosenberg concluded that the *"Vietnam War has become a benchmark for what not to do in all future US foreign conflicts."* [Italics mine.]

I was thirty-two years old at the outset of the Vietnam War. Like the politicians of the day, I also objected to the protests and flag burnings that ensued. I was conditioned to believe that any protest of the government was without merit and not justified. Instead of *Father Knows Best,* as the simplistic TV show was called, it was "Our Government Knows Best." I rationalized my Vietnam perception in this way: The people in charge, our government, are there to protect us, the American people. They were in a much better position to assess the situation accurately, because they were privy to classified and secret information about the war, which, of course wasn't available to me. Besides, who was I to question authority under those circumstances? Looking at our past history, with the exception of the Korean War, our country was always victorious, which, by definition, made the politicians' choice to go to war the right one. Like a naïve schoolboy, I believed that America was, by definition, *the good guy* in any wars we fought.

Today, with my understanding of what happened to our country during and after the Vietnam War, I would not have supported the war. Not only would I have not supported it, but I also would have taken steps to express my dismay over what had happened to our political parties in ignoring the views of the people, just like I'm doing now in two political books here in the twenty-first century.

I think in each of our lives, when our sense of integrity and its dictates or the principles we live by are being threatened sufficiently that we feel we must act, we must then do something. And it is then that we must not only "talk the talk," as the saying goes, but also "walk the walk." The only reason I do that is to respond to my sense of integrity. When it's being threatened by being insulted by outside events, we all need to rise to the occasion and respond to its dictates. That's precisely what our Founding Fathers and their countrymen did after they realized they had tolerated enough abuse leading up to the Revolutionary War. They simply weren't going to take it anymore, because what the British were doing was insulting and abusing the colonists' integrity.

There were other reasons I would have changed my mind, besides what I've already mentioned. They were:

1. Over the years, perhaps I've acquired a bit more maturity of judgment, and my ability to trust myself to make good decisions, independent of others' actions, has also grown.
2. Over the years, I've learned the importance of delving into my soul and recognizing what's important to me by my being better able to realize what my integrity is all about. This includes deepening my understanding that empathy—hence compassion—in addition to my personal integrity are two of the greatest gifts God has given each of us. That's so, because by using our integrity and

compassion, we can better understand how others' experience fits—or doesn't fit—into our own belief systems.

3. Out of those kinds of experiences, I have developed wisdom, which, according to our Founding Fathers, should be fostered through education.

Wisdom is acquired through knowledge and experience. The reason our Founding Fathers felt wisdom was important for every citizen to develop is that it helps us to understand why a course of action should or should not be followed. And of course, through a thorough knowledge of our country's history, we can better understand what actions worked and what didn't; hence, we would know how to avoid repeating the history we don't wish to repeat.

One of the main reasons the Founding Fathers and their countrymen were successful in vanquishing the British and winning the Revolutionary War, was because through their wisdom, acquired by knowledge and experience, the colonists, as a community of like-minded thinkers, were painfully aware of the many taxation abuses the British had bestowed upon them; by living through that period, they knew it was *important* to do something; they knew which actions hadn't worked, so that by the time war happened, it was the only thing left to do if they were going to protect their collective integrity, even if it meant losing their properties and lives to do so.

Clearly, since the Vietnam protests, our elected politicians, who should be protecting us and representing our concerns, have overridden our interests in favor of their parties' agendas, or misguided understanding of what the real political and country's cares should be. That's because our democratic process, which is at the core of how our country's decisions are made, have been trumped in favor of what's currently popular or will attract the most votes to get the politician reelected. Therefore, what has *not* been utilized in a way that our political representatives, and us, the common Americans, should be represented, but aren't, are not only our concerns and anxieties, but also what our country expects from us. For, what we think our government should be concerned with, and what they seem to feel is important to them and the country, are at odds. Neither party represents the values that we, the common Americans, believe are important to protect so much that we'd be willing to give up our treasure or our lives to defend. All our country wants are transparent reasons for why we, the American people, should make the sacrifices our politicians, hence, our government, wants us to make.

Unfortunately, the speed our country is going down those tracks has accelerated with each passing year. This has caused our nation to become more in debt and financially beholden to friendly and unfriendly countries alike. In order to maintain our standard of living, which is declining with each passing year, we have had to sacrifice our sense of integrity by being dishonest with ourselves and others. As a result, we have had to compromise our values and principles in order to try to hold constant our ever-slipping standard of living.

Fame and Fortune

Today, *the "almighty" dollar* has taken center stage at representing the pinnacle of success and the thing we should treasure in this country above anything else. In that sense, for more than a few people, the attainment of money and material wealth has become an opiate to an addict, turning the act of accumulating wealth for one's own satisfaction into a preoccupation, an obsession, and a driving force in itself, replacing all else as the primary reason for living. For those kinds of people, motivated by greed and avarice, the more money they can accrue, and the more material goods they can accumulate, the more successful they feel they are—not only in their own eyes but society's as well.

On our media, we are daily bombarded with how we can gain fame and fortune, mostly through advertising, but also in entertainment and "reality" content on TV, radio, and the Internet; in movies, newspapers, and magazines; and in the mail through a variety of print sources. The fame-and-fortune message has become so prevalent that Americans have become brainwashed into thinking a goal of mere wealth is to be valued, even if our integrity at an individual and national level is being endangered.

I say "national level" because many movers and shakers and influential politicians who are in a position to influence the formulation of governmental policy view the *wealth* of our nation as its standard of excellence. It is common among them to cite how our brand of capitalism reigns supreme when compared to any other economic system that exists in the world. In fact, our brand of capitalism is conflated with our brand of democracy as if these words were synonymous, when in fact capitalism is an economics system not a type of republic.

However, should financial attainment alone necessarily be the gauge of a nation's *worth?* I believe not. There is indeed much more to life than making money. At my old age, I have learned that rather than the attainment of money or material goods as a measure of success, the most treasured thing to me are relationships. It's the ability to be of service to others and help those in need that is a measure of my worth. Not the dollar value, but the human caring and loving component, which is the true measure of a man's or a woman's significance.

To put it in political terms, it's what politicians can do for their fellow citizens that is the mark of a true statesman or stateswoman, and on a grander scale, the lasting impact their efforts have on our country as a whole to make this country a better place to live in for all those who are privileged to be a part of this great nation.

For what has been sacrificed over the years to attain such a goal? Answer: The price we've paid for such questionable acclaim has been the loss of our own self-respect. In addition, our nation has lost the adulation and admiration other countries have shown us since shortly after the Second World War. If Americans use their country's integrity as a measure of its worth and then assess its worth against that gold standard, it would be hard not to conclude we have fallen far short of what we should value, here, in these United States.

Our moral compass is what went askew to cause us to be in the pickle that our country is in today. Over the years, our government has veered further and further away from what we as a country should have valued. And that is the ideals that our Founding Fathers and all the other battles weary soldiers fought to protect, namely our freedom and our country's integrity—or the feeling that comes when you know what you're doing— or have done—is the right thing to do, even if you risk your life doing it.

As I write this, I am reminded that we've been in this moral compass pickle since the birth of our great nation. The only difference is that today, more people and more economic classes are being impacted by immoral treatment by our government. The reason I'm much more aware of this now is because the middle class, which I'm a part of, is being affected.

It's human nature to not become involved in things that don't affect you personally. That's why education is so important if our republic will be saved. Education enlightens Americans and enhances the voting public to make good choices. Ignorance fosters narrow-mindedness and prejudice, because without learning and understanding, you cannot know why you should make the voting choices that you make, resulting in a lack of critical thinking. That is the purpose of education.

Let's stroll down memory lane and refresh ourselves with the gross injustices and immorality that has existed since our country was born:

- *Not one agreement* has been honored with our indigenous population—ever—every treaty broken or meddled with, even as recently as at the time of this writing.
- Reparations promised for the damage done to the self-esteem and social structures of African Americans through slavery (not to mention payment for building much of the country's infrastructure) were never paid. Yes, promised. As a result of the Emancipation Proclamation, during the last stages of the Civil War in 1865, "forty acres of arable land and a mule" were going to be provided to former slaves who had become free as a result of the advance of the Union armies into the territory previously controlled by the Confederacy. However, after President Lincoln's assassination, his successor, President Andrew Johnson rescinded the order and returned all the land to its previous white owners, giving the landless, penniless, but suddenly free blacks nothing.
- The Women's Suffrage Movement lasted from 1848 until 1920, when thousands of courageous women marched in the streets.

They had to endure beatings and hunger strikes, and submitted to arrest and jail in order to gain the right to vote.

• The introduction of labor laws and unions occurred in 1833 when the first state child-labor laws were introduced. A high school textbook passage entitled "Child Labor in Factories," reports the following: "Children as young as six years old during the industrial revolution worked hard hours for little or no pay. Children sometimes worked up to 19 hours a day, with a one-hour total break. This was a little bit on the extreme, but it was not common for children who worked in factories to work 12–14 hours with the same minimal breaks. Not only were these children subject to long hours, but also, they were in horrible conditions. Large, heavy, and dangerous equipment was very common for children to be using or working near. Many accidents occurred injuring or killing children on the job. Not until the Factory Act of 1833 did things improve. Children were paid only a fraction of what an adult would get, and sometimes factory owners would get away with paying them nothing. Orphans were the ones subject to this slave-like labor. The factory owners justified their absence of payroll by saying that they gave the orphans food, shelter, and clothing, all of which were far below par. The children who did get paid were paid very little."[48]

• Over the history of the labor unions, workers were paid as little as employers could get away with, no matter the level of profit, until the labor movement brought unions and laws to bear—which have been rescinded bit by bit since 1980, bringing us to the present version of that earlier robber-baron era, which is a term that applies to unscrupulous and powerful nineteenth-century businessmen who used unethical or, at best, questionable business practices to amass their fortunes. An example of such practices from that time is setting a product at a very low price to drive

---

[48] Needham, Massachusetts, Public Schools curriculum website, Needham High School, http://www2.needham.k12.ma.us/nhs/cur/Baker_00/2002_p7/ak_p7/childlabor.html.

out competing businesses, and paying the worker very low wages in order to do that. The businesses that were affected eventually couldn't compete, because the prices were too low to make a profit. At that point, the robber baron would step in and buy them out. Once there was no competition, they would again raise the price of the goods far above the original levels. This is again common practice.

There are many other examples I could give to illustrate where capitalism's ethical practices have gone astray. I hope what I shared with you helps you understand that, although current offenses have not been as monumental as they have been in times past—largely because of the labor protections still in place—with each passing year, criminal behavior on the part of corporations and now, government, are becoming more and more egregious, to the point where, because of the people's anger, a major, violent uprising may ensue, as has occurred numerous times in the past, unless a sense of fairness between the worker and the employer, between the voter and the politician occurs—where compromises are made and laws get passed that benefit *everyone,* not just the rich and powerful, and other special-interest groups.

Our forefathers knew that the powerful always have issues with integrity; the powerful try to get away with whatever they can *when no one is looking.* This is what our Constitution was written to guard against, as imperfectly as it has been upheld. But now the ones who are suffering from that lack of integrity have spread up the food chain—middle-class white men are suffering along with the historically subjugated African Americans, Native Americans, immigrants, women of all classes and ethnicities, and same-sex-oriented couples. But the Constitution remains on the side of the people.

Perhaps that is why our politicians are ignoring us today—because they have always gotten away with it before (since King George III, that is). The question is, will they now? As we approach the time when our electorate will be majority nonwhite, will their next move be to try to get rid of the one person–one vote guarantee in national elections?

Let's take a look and see what went askew to cause such a disparity between what we'd like to see America be compared to what it has become.

Although politics being used in blatant and self-serving manners was not nearly as apparent during the Revolutionary War as it is today in the twenty-first century, the seeds of capitalism, the competitive spirit, and survival-of-the-fittest kind of philosophy had already been sown during the Revolutionary War.

Because of their absence of public virtue, our young country's capitalists allowed their interest in financial gain to take precedence over their duty to respond to the common good. Rather than the colonies cooperating with one another for the greater good, which was to defeat British tyranny, they neglected the needs of the Revolutionary Army, which resulted in the soldiers being inadequately clothed and fed to the point where they nearly starved and froze to death. Instead of helping Washington's army defeat the British, the colonies' bodies of government competed with one another, one colony against another, for trade superiority and financial gain. This all being done at the Continental Army's expense.

By the end of the Revolutionary War, I believe the values related to honesty, morality (integrity), qualities such as empathy and compassion, as well as other behaviors that reflect the goodness of people, were incorporated into the Founding Fathers' psyches, and by extension into the whole of America's psyche. The process of building the framework to contain a new nation based on the ideals of liberty and equality created that collective psyche for the foundation of future generations. The selfish, self-serving, narcissistic qualities that seem to characterize our culture today were not as dominant in the 1700s; we need to focus on rebuilding the character that made the vision expressed in those foundational documents possible.

CHAPTER 8

ISSUES IN TODAY'S POLITICS

Today, we know politicians have little allegiance and loyalty to the concept of public virtue. As soon as they are elected, their main concern is what they must do to be reelected.

When you're a politician, you take sides on issues based on opinions and biases (prejudices). If you continue to think and act on your own biases only and believe what you think is on the *right side of the argument,* the less likely you'll be persuaded to temper that view and compromise for legislation to get passed.

It's the same sort of thing that happens when you favor one limb over another. Say you injured your leg; depending on which one was hurt, right or left, that's the one you're going to favor. The more you favor that limb, the less inclined you're going to be to pay attention to the healthy leg. Until you wear it out.

The same is true in the world of politics. If you favor the left or right side of the political spectrum, your political leanings will be in keeping with either the Democratic Party or Republican Party, respectively. The harder you lean to the left over the right—and vice versa—the less likely you will be to reconsider your position and adjust it toward the middle of the range. And you most certainly have to move one way or the other to be able to compromise!

We have to look at psychology's *cognitive dissonance theory* in order to understand why this entrenchment happens.

Cognitive Dissonance

One would think that common interest would be enough to spur the two parties to achieve resolution of the issues before them. One would think a shared belief in their importance to our nation would motivate our legislators to achieve a compromise on these issues, so legislation addressing a solution could be put into law posthaste. It's fair to assume that their sense of responsibility would mean they'd have no trouble compromising. But if you think or assume any of these things, you'd be wrong!

How can that be? The explanation can be found when we look at the part cognitive thinking plays in our everyday life: We use it every time we think of something. We are influenced by how we feel about our *previous* thoughts and feelings related to what we're thinking about *now.* These thoughts and feelings are stored up in our unconscious mind, some in our preconscious mind—or just below the level of awareness—and some are further down again, where we have to reflect long and hard before we can dredge them up and make them conscious. Our thoughts and feelings have to be conscious, on the surface, and easily recalled immediately, before we can actually think about something. But when our unconscious, preconceived notions and old reactions—that which is stored in our heads—conflict with new information and current experiences, it causes a kind of mental discomfort that we call *cognitive dissonance.*

The trouble is, what was stored in the heads of our Founding Fathers and their fellow colonists is not comparable to what is in the minds of Americans of the twenty-first century. That's because inside today's Americans' political heads is where political *garbage* is housed. These are the bits and pieces of political rhetoric and meaningless associations that have been stored in the unconsciousness from sound bites and misinformation over time. While the colonists' mental inventory was primarily free of political nonsense, our unconscious political storage bins are filled with political half-truths, bold falsehoods, and vitriolic statements about the opposing political parties' makeup. Constant repetition of this garbage is stored where we aren't even aware of its existence. And it influences how we think about our politics and that of the opposition.

On the other hand, the colonists' decisions were based on their current perceptual attitudes as history was unfolding before them. All they had to do was compare their present circumstances with their mother England's past, and then move forward; they knew they wanted something different.

In our time, however, cognitive dissonance ("mental tapes") seems to be omnipresent in internal and external dialogue, so it is most certainly important to understand its role in political discourse. It takes courage to mine your own thoughts for the outdated stuff you are holding onto from the past and then to test it against new information, present conditions, and current thinking on the issues. If our leaders today do not show the same courage our forefather's demonstrated in forging the new nation, we are sunk going forward now.

Because cognitive dissonance is a central dynamic to each of our thought processes, and most certainly is front and center in political thought, at the point you decide I have a political view that differs significantly from yours, the odds are that you won't continue to read this book, or if you do, you won't do it with a glad heart because you won't be reading with an open mind. That's because of your political bias and your assumptions about mine. You will already have a preconceived idea of what's wrong and what needs to be done to fix the system, and when you hear a contrary opinion, *cognitive dissonance* is created, which is a painful form of anxiety and nervousness that results from a conflict of needs and ideas. *The normal reaction is to mitigate the facts in order to hold onto the beliefs!* This makes solving certain issues in the country most difficult.

Because of the angst that happens, it's human nature to not really hear, let alone accept, points of view different from our own. In order to develop an open mind, where we listen to *all* sides of an issue, we need to understand the unconscious dynamics in play within ourselves to prevent shutting down our ears, hearts, and minds.

When someone expresses points of view different from our own, particularly if the subject is religion or politics, the degree to which we are wedded to those concepts will determine the degree of apprehension we'll experience. Furthermore, the more definitively that contrary view is expressed, the more likely we are to take personal affront at the challenge to our own value systems or beliefs.

Obviously, the stronger you feel that what you believe is true, the less likely you're going to be willing to budge from your original stance and the more severe your cognitive dissonance if the facts don't match the beliefs. That's why, in the case of politics, you don't see many extreme conservatives hanging out with flaming liberals. Neither can take the heat.

Cognitive dissonance theory helps explain why the longer you stick with your political position and embrace that belief in toto, the more dogmatic you become in believing that what you embrace is the correct position. That's because you will never take the time, either consciously or unconsciously, to let yourself hear the other side of the argument. The reason this closed-minded thinking occurs is that a willingness to hear all sides of the issue would cause too much anxiety and apprehension, something your ego tries to avoid whenever possible. Therefore, it's just more comfortable and less anxiety producing to embrace the one side that you're convinced is the truth with a capital T—rather than examine any other side of the discussion. If it's political thought or any belief system that you're discussing that differs from another whom you're having the discussion with, *and* you are feeling agitation, chances are you are experiencing cognitive dissonance. Rather than getting mad, you could take it as a sign that the other side's facts don't jibe with your feelings. Check out the facts. If they're true, it might be your beliefs that need the adjustment.

This might be why it is difficult for politicians to maintain their integrity. There are many times on the campaign trail when they need to listen to and be responsive to points of view that are contrary to what they believe. It's very possible that what's said makes as much political sense as their own position does if they are listening with empathy and allowing themselves to put themselves in the shoes of their constituents. But if politicians feel bound to particular political party positions and can't be empathetic with or compassionate to views and situations different from their own, much less adjust their positions when they learn something new, then they will have a problem with us. And we with them. Because as Americans, we need to trust that our representatives will consider our views and needs and not just their own or their party's.

In order to reach the entire electorate and respond to all the needs of the citizenry that comprise this great country of ours, there are many times when politicians must throw away their ideological preferences, and vote from their hearts as well as their minds. Those times are when it would be unfair to only exercise the intellectual side of the argument, when what needs to be employed is the empathetic and compassionate side as well. That's because our integrity or character derives from the *feeling* side of our psyches and resides in our unconsciousness; it is the part of our personalities that, metaphorically, speaks from our heart.

Bipartisan Issues That Need Fixing

Throughout this treatise, I've tried to make my *discussion* of politics as nonpolitical as possible. In other words, the kind of politics I cared to focus on are the kind of noncontroversial political issues that, regardless of whether you are a Republican, a Democrat, or an independent, you would agree with the spirit and the intent of what's being expressed—concluding that, because it has at its base, a thought, policy, or an idea that would be good for all Americans, it would be worthy of adoption.

However, based on our glimpse of America's current state, it's not difficult to identify several issues that need to be addressed. These issues can only be resolved if our two political parties arrive at some kind of compromise so legislation gets passed and the country's business gets done—not for the good of the parties, but rather, for the good of the American citizens.

The issues are:

1. Respecting the need to **revise the tax code** so it's fairer and equitable. Expecting everyone who is able to pay their fair share of taxes to do so. The consequences of continuing the congressional deadlock where the wealthy are not paying their fair share of taxes is not only selfish but, frankly, immoral. It's immoral or dishonest because the congressional members who swear to defend and uphold the constitutional dictates are not doing that when they refuse to pay their fair share of taxes. Since the Sixteenth Amendment allows Congress to levy an income tax, implied in that responsibility is that the tax structure reflect that those who receive more yearly monetary gain, should pay proportionally more taxes to reflect that gain. Those who earn more money are expected to pay their fair share of taxes, proportional to their income level, just like every other American citizen must do. *The democratic process is based on fairness.* When fellow Americans see that any group, rich or poor, are taking advantage of our marvelous system of government, where fairness is not operating, they get fighting mad. That is why, to a large extent, the Wall Street demonstrators, the 99 percenters, have taken to the streets and parks throughout the country—because the wealthy are indeed not paying their fair share of taxes, considering their income levels.

The Founding Fathers recognized that freedom comes at a price. They believed that those who can give more should pay more. That's the small price, relative to their wealth, that we pay for, having been given the opportunity to live in this country and enjoy the additional benefits the wealthy are able to experience.

All of the conveniences that we experience daily, from the construction of roads and bridges to postal services, emergency response services, and the various entitlement programs that are available to every eligible voter have to be financed; that means taxes have to be collected to pay for such ventures.

To make the tax code appear fairer for everyone concerned—and so the rich don't feel they are being taken advantage of—perhaps some tax should be levied on every household, regardless how little that might be, even if the tax per year is $100, $50, or $25 per year. If we're all in this together, shouldn't we all, as Americans, contribute something to show our appreciation for being able to live in this marvelous country of ours and avail ourselves of all the freedoms that our forefathers so valiantly fought to protect from British tyranny and oppression?

We must remember that we all pay sales tax and gas tax, and other regressive taxes abound, which are equally paid for by poor and rich alike. Anyone who has a job is paying taxes.

My point is that it's easy to *assume* people who are poor, whether they're employed or not, don't pay taxes. But, as stated earlier, that's just not true. Even though everyone pay taxes of one kind or another, what is frequently overlooked is because they may not pay any income tax, it's frequently assumed that they are not paying their fair share of taxes.

Paying taxes has become the gold standard in assuming that people who pay taxes are contributing to the general welfare of our nation's future, regardless of how little that payment may be.

That's true not only for the poor, but the wealthy as well. What we, as Americans, want our citizenry to do is pay their *fair* share of taxes. That not only applies to the poor, but the rich alike. The poor may really have to scrape to find the means to pay the graduated taxes assigned to their income level. That's because, based on the benefits they received from the government as well as any employment they might have had during that taxable year, it may not be easy for them to pay the taxes. Most certainly not as easy as compared to those who can well afford to pay the taxes assigned to their much higher tax bracket.

2. Address the national debt: "The Outstanding Public Debt as of 26 February 2012 at 12:24: 33 AM GMT," according to the US National Debt Clock is "$15,444,039,698,920.73." That's fifteen trillion, four hundred forty-four billion, thirty-nine million, six hundred ninety-eight thousand, nine hundred twenty dollars and seventy-three cents. The estimated population of the United States as of this writing is 312,292,131, so *each American citizen's share of this debt is $49,4563.97.* The national debt has continued to increase an average of four billion dollars per day since September 28, 2007!

It's obvious that our generation and many more generations to come will be unable to balance the budget, so I don't expect it to be balanced in the immediate or even distant future. But hopefully, sometime.

Since to fund the debt requires a two-thirds' majority vote in the Senate and three-quarters in the House of Representatives, our members of Congress need to work together, setting aside their political and party differences, to do what's right for the American people in developing a plan to reduce the national debt that is equitable and fair.

It's possible our Founding Fathers would be appalled at the current level of debt our country operates under. One of the reasons they wrote the Constitution to replace the Articles of Confederation was that they did not have a federally run monetary policy. Prior to writing it, the Congress of the Confederation had no power to tax and thus no clear way to raise the money to repay war debts. This lack of a stable source of funding had made it difficult for the Continental Army to both obtain its necessary provisions and pay its soldiers. During the war, and for some time after, Congress obtained what funds it could from subsidies granted by the king of France, from aid requested from the states but received from only a few, and from European loans.

The way the Constitution was written allowed the federal government to levy taxes and issue bonds to pay outstanding debts incurred as monies lent to America to fund the needs of General Washington's army.

At the time, Alexander Hamilton, Washington's treasury secretary, urged prompt payment of the debt, stating, "Among ourselves, the most enlightened friends of good government, are those whose expectations of prompt payment are the highest."

The United States has had debt since its inception. Government records show that debts incurred during the American Revolutionary War amounted to $75,463,476.52 by January 1, 1791. Over the following forty-five years, the debt grew. Then, under President Andrew Jackson, the public debt actually shrank to zero by January 1835. Soon after, however, it grew into the millions again and has continued to grow.

3. Issue three is the need to contain all wasteful spending, starting by eliminating earmarked spending. Earmarks are aspects of government spending that are reserved by law for a particular use. The original idea was to make sure enough money would be allocated for a specific use. However, it should be outlawed, because it is used more than not for *pork-barrel projects,* which are those designed to benefit only people in a particular part of the country—and more particularly, to fatten the political careers of their elected officials. Although both sides of the aisle are guilty of earmarking and putting into law pork and waste that our whole country is then obligated to pay, Alaska's so-called *Bridge to*

Nowhere went beyond the pale. Fortunately, it was ultimately withdrawn from consideration.

Bills that are up for passage should be considered on their own merits rather than because pork-barrel projects are tacked onto them to sweeten the deal for a politician's vote. That's not the kind of *legislative compromise* that we need to get bills passed. What we need is honest debate between both parties working toward an *amicable compromise* so that any particular bill ultimately gets passed by the Congress and signed by the president. This would force politicians to either support or reject a bill for the right reason. *There can be a big difference between doing something for the right reason vs. for the political reason.* Only the right action would demonstrate to the American public that politicians can indeed work together to do the people's business.

4. Job creation. Improvement is needed in the jobs available for the currently unemployed. Too many of them do not indeed provide *a living wage.* Trading Economics, a statistical website for international economic data, shows that while unemployment has been reduced from 9.6 percent in 2010 to 8.3 percent by the end of January 2012, a significant drop, we still have a ways to go.[49] The data also indicate that from 1948 until 2010 the United States' unemployment rate averaged 5.7 percent, reaching an historical high of 10.8 percent in November 1982.

Rather than both political parties rejoicing on the significance of the reduction of the unemployment numbers, regardless of what political party's president was in power at the time, the opposition party inevitably looks at the glass as being half-*empty*, rather than half-*full*. We no longer think of the individuals who have contributed to legislative victories, but rather, which political party got the credit. That makes any bipartisan effort hard to complete. Look at McCain-Feingold. Crafted in the old style by two statesmen sitting across the aisle from one another, the campaign-finance-reform law passed but was never able to get legs to stand on as neither party could claim it. In the end, it was, arguably, killed by the Supreme

---

[49] Trading Economics, "United States Unemployment Rate," http://www.tradingeconomics.com/united-states/unemployment-rate.

Court's Republican-backed Citizens United decision. In that sense, our political parties have hijacked our political system. Politicians' allegiances on both sides of the aisle have become focused on their respective parties and not on individuals searching their minds and hearts. The result is that the individual is absolved from taking responsibility for his or her political deeds and misdeeds, for it's the party that did it.

There were no political parties when Washington was president. That was just fine with him; he felt they could become a detriment in doing the people's business. Rather than listening to the electorate and determining, on that basis, what's best for the country, politicians too easily allow the politics of the day to have an undue influence in determining the political agenda for the country.

5. Campaign-finance reform. Realizing the millions of dollars necessary to run for public office, clearly, campaign-finance reform is long overdue.

Dave Gilson, writing for *Mother Jones* Magazine online, wrote an article entitled "The Crazy Cost of Becoming President, from Lincoln to Obama." He mentioned that President Obama spent $730 million in his 2008 campaign in order to defeat Senator McCain. This year, 2012, it's estimated he will spend at least "$1 billion" to beat his Republican rival.

When we compare the $730 million spent to get President Obama elected in the year 2008, and compare it to President G. W. Bush to be reelected four years earlier, according to Gilson, it cost President Obama "twice as much" as what President Bush spent to beat Senator Kerry. And, Gilson states, Obama's cost to be elected president was "260 times" more compared to what President Abraham Lincoln spent in his first election (as measured in 2011 dollars).

So, at the moment, the upcoming 2012 contest between President Obama and his Republican presidential opponent—which looks at this writing before the convention to be Mitt Romney—may prove to be the most expensive ever.

That's not beyond the realm of possibility since there's a new ingredient that has recently been added to the campaign-cost mix, and that's the introduction of super-PAC monies, which I feel, quite frankly, is something that never should have been passed by our Supreme Court.

Tom Murse, writing for About.com in his article entitled "The Citizens United Ruling: A Primer on the Landmark Court Case," writes that it is a "political-action committee that is allowed to raise and spend unlimited amounts of money from corporations, unions, individuals, and associations."[50] The PAC's role, he says, is "similar to that of traditional political-action committees. They advocate for the election or defeat of candidates for federal office by purchasing television, radio and print advertisements, and other media."

Traditionally, candidates could accept $2,500 from each individual donor per election. That means $5,000 can be expended per election year—half in the primary and half in the general election. But that's the limit! With super PACs, unlimited monies may be expended to elect or defeat candidates. The restrictions are placed on candidates and traditional candidate committees—they can't receive monies *directly* from a super PAC.

The reason the super PACs are so controversial is that the contribution of big money to candidates will inevitably lead to corruption and scandal, because of the inequality that's at the heart of its very nature. It gives a decided and significant advantage to the recipients of these super-PAC donations who receive a disproportionately larger total amount of donations than the other candidates who don't receive any, or, if they do, a disproportionately smaller amount of monies from super-PAC donations. Ultimately, the scandal comes by the election being decided by the amount of monies that a candidate can raise over the various candidates' campaign rhetoric. The super PACs are a good example of the old expression "Put your money where your mouth is"; it's a slogan that is not appropriate to use in political campaigns.

Murse reports, "In writing his dissenting opinion for the Supreme Court, Justice John Paul Stevens opined of the majority: 'At bottom, the Court's opinion is thus a rejection of the common sense of the American people, who have recognized a need to prevent corporations from undermining self-government since the founding, and who have fought

---

[50] http://uspolitics.about.com/od/fi rstamendment/a/Citizens-United.htm.

against the distinctive corrupting potential of corporate electioneering since the days of Theodore Roosevelt.'" Frankly, I would rather have had Chief Justice John G. Roberts make that statement, since I would then feel his Supreme Court was on the right side of the argument.

6. Immigration Reform. There is a case to be made that our laws should be enforced and that illegal immigrants who break the law to come here should be deported. However, to summarily decide to deport them for that reason alone is both specious and unsustainable. That's because the length of time someone has been in the United States needs to be considered, and the relationship that exists between them and the businesses that benefit from the work of cheap labor needs to be assessed. Some of those workers have gone on to join churches, send their children to public schools, and become a part of their community. Displacing them now does not make sense morally or economically. Instead, if the workers who have been in this country for many years, have no criminal record and agree to pay back taxes and a fine, they should be given an opportunity to apply for permanent citizenship. They should *not* be allowed to skip legal immigration, as they should eventually be able to earn that right.

There is indeed an ethical question to this discussion. We have a moral obligation, where it's a matter of conscience, to help immigrants who fit the scenarios I've just described stay in this country by allowing them a means to obtain citizenship.

The more the issue of immigration becomes a political football, where the support of it is a means to secure the Latino or any other nationality's immigration vote, the more we dehumanize the whole immigration process and cheapen the real reason for helping the immigrant become a full-fledged citizen of these United States. The reason being, it's the right thing to do.

The Founding Fathers welcomed legal immigrants with open arms. Our country's strength and heritage is based on all those who have immigrated to this country in their efforts to seek freedom, work, and options in their pursuit of happiness. Wouldn't the Founding Fathers urge the politicians of today to use the family as their model as they did in treating the immigrants in their earlier century? Aren't these the same principles and beliefs that they incorporated into the Constitution? Wouldn't they treat the immigrant in the same way they would wish to be treated, that being with integrity—with honesty and respect? Wouldn't they expect the immigrant to follow the very same code of conduct for living in America as the rest of our community of families, and to follow the principles as stated in our country's Constitution, just like every other American is supposed to follow?

7. Improve our educational system. Our nation's strength is dependent on our children's educational future. Frankly, it shouldn't be a political issue, for the answer should be that all Americans want the best education for their country's future, which is their children.

There's a great danger that the two political parties and the teacher's union, in an effort to seek votes for their own personal agendas, have already commandeered our educational issues. Education is being used as a political football where nothing gets resolved satisfactorily as long as the two political parties and the teachers' unions are unable to come to a happy compromise whereby legislation is passed that enhances the school system and benefits all of our nation's children.

Clearly, our Founding Fathers would be absolutely dismayed at how political our school systems have become. For example, instead of debating the merits of charter vs. public schools, and home schooling vs. receiving a public education, and which curricula is superior, wouldn't they urge all schools to have integrated courses of academic study, emphasizing *how* to think, not what to think, which was very much attuned to Thomas Jefferson's thoughts on education?

With respect to *how* to think, considering the kinds of intellectual stimulation that seems so all encompassing in our twenty-first-century culture today, where such stimulation is externally driven rather than internally determined, it would seem that our Founding Fathers would urge our school systems to teach their students, as early as possible, the value and joy of reading as a means of acquiring knowledge and understanding of the world around them. And in the process of doing that help their students learn how to think analytically and critically as they develop the delight of exercising their brains by reading for reading's sake. Reading just to read stimulates their imaginations and thought processes as they empathize with the characters in the book. The effort also stimulates the production of internal thoughts and images as opposed to passively responding to external stimulation where there is little opportunity to enjoy the act of thinking and creating thoughts and ideas.

I believe the Founding Fathers would be dismayed at how our twenty-first-century society has moved from one that valued analytical thought and critical thinking to one that emphasizes instant gratification, entertainment, consumerism, and narcissism.

Up to the middle of the twentieth century, the primary external stimulus to obtain information was print media, then the telephone, and then radio. Aside from vocal communication, those external information-gathering means did *not* significantly interrupt our reasoning powers, which had been the modus operandi to process information and influence thought, values, and socio-moral standards and ideals for centuries.

Now, with the advent of television, and more recently, the development of the Internet and computerized and text-messaging devices, our society has been replaced from being an *internal thought–driven society to an external, visually stimulated culture.* What that encourages is passivity— where we busy ourselves *taking in* information and responding to the messages and information that constantly bombard our senses, where our valuable time is *taken up* either responding to others' text messages, or, because of our addiction to TV, watching excessive amounts of it. Additionally, we are constantly being bombarded with what kinds of things we should buy to make our lives more complete and fulfilled. All this is at the expense of reflection, contemplation, and introspection, where we use critical thinking and analytical reasoning to solve problems and make good political decisions based on sound logic and examination.

Unless our cultural values return to the period where we as a society cherish our mind for what it can empower each of us to become, which is to be responsive to society's concerns in general and individuals' needs in particular, we will soon have developed citizens who will do what's intellectually the most expedient and easiest thing to do, which is either to not vote at all, or if it's done, use little or no thoughtful critical judgment in the kinds of voting judgments made. That's because those people have never trained their minds to think analytically and critically. It is for that reason, they will show limited intellectual ability and/or interest in dealing with abstract concepts. Their narcissism, self-centeredness, and entertainment-driven desires will have trumped their ability to actively and intelligently participate in the election processes where good political judgments are made in choosing the most worthy political candidates to serve this great nation of ours.

The Founding Fathers would urge that each school educate their students *how to be good people* and citizens of this marvelous country of ours and encourage them to become other-centered by becoming involved in the community and the country. They would expect young people to learn that it is their duty to work toward something greater than themselves. They most certainly would urge the study of American history and why this country developed the form of government that it did.

I also believe they would urge each school system to understand why the American Revolution occurred, why the Declaration of Independence, the Constitution, and Bill of Rights were written, and why those documents have stood the test of time.

The Founding Fathers recognized the frailties that come from being human. They realized that we are by nature selfish and seek our own pleasures at the expense of others. Our Founding Fathers realized that in order to govern ourselves—ensuring a sufficient amount of order in our lives and that the rule of law can optimally flourish—each American citizen needs to be able to use his or her integrity, which is part of his or her soul, in such a way that helps the group govern itself.

Since being able to live a life sufficiently disciplined that no public order is necessary is impossible for most people to do, some degree of *public order* through government and rule of law is required. But in order for our society to operate optimally and for our citizens to thrive, education is necessary to achieve societal order through limited government. The kind of education is very special, for the founders emphasized not only the classical liberal arts education, which they themselves had and which helped them attain wisdom, so important in governing their republic, but also they learned how important being a good person and putting country before self was in sustaining and maintaining public order with *minimal* governmental interference. For it was the very incorporation of those virtues in their individual souls and what formed their individual senses of integrity, that made their new republic and the liberty that the Constitution affords possible.

I wouldn't expect our modern school systems to necessarily offer a *classical* liberal arts education, which would include the study of Greek and Roman literature in the original languages, the kind of education our Founding Fathers received, though that education undoubtedly informed and facilitated their vision of governance for the new republic. Wisdom can be still be drawn from the classics by reading translations and discussions of these ancient works in modern English. But these and even later societies must be studied in order to learn what worked in those original Western republics and what didn't. The history and literature of previous experiments in republican forms of government will help the discerning citizen understand what we need to know about our own.

8. **Energy independence.** We have struggled with energy independence since Richard Nixon was president. "Let this be our national goal," said Nixon in his 1974 State of the Union address, "At the end of this decade, in the year 1980, the United States will not be dependent on any other country for the energy we need."

Well, that obviously has not been the case. It was marvelous political rhetoric, but that's about the extent of it.

I believe our Founding Fathers would have anticipated the energy problem sooner than we have done. After doing so, they would have acted in concert with the community and their fellow political statesmen to fix the problem. Because of their love and respect for one another and their country, and because they would have made the hard choices in a democratic way, a very public way, all the citizens of America would clearly understand the problem and its solution. That would be done because they and their communities would have been other-centered and eager to work toward something greater than themselves. Therefore, they would have been willing to make whatever sacrifices necessary to sustain themselves until a solution could be realized.

I make these suppositions because our country was founded with love, empathy, compassion, and integrity in the hearts of our Founding Fathers and their fellow countrymen, who realized those were the unbeatable ingredients required to overcome any future obstacles that might stand in the way of maintaining the freedoms that they so valiantly earned when they fought the Revolutionary War.

9. Issue nine refers to how to deal with **entitlement programs** equitably. The examples of entitlement programs at the federal level in the United States that need "fixing," include Social Security, Medicare, and Medicaid, most Veterans' Administration programs, federal employee and military retirement plans, unemployment compensation, food stamps, and agricultural price-support programs.

Considering that most states and federal government programs don't have the finances to adequately fund these entitlement programs, there has to be personal financial sacrifices made by each American voting citizen if our entitlement programs are not to become bankrupt to the point where, at best, only a paltry amount of payouts may be possible.

No politician wants to cut entitlement programs, for fear he or she will alienate the voting public. However, because our Founding Fathers believed in making decisions using the democratic process, where laws are passed because compromises are made by everybody, and since during Washington's presidency there were no political parties, they would urge their representatives from the various states, and the president, to do what's best for not only their political constituents, but also for the nation as a whole, in spite of their reluctance to do so. Therefore, they would be urged to follow their senses of integrity, their caring for one another and all Americans, and make the hard choices by acting like statesmen and stateswomen, and pass laws that need to be passed.

We should recognize that the survival of entitlement programs requires greater financial sacrifice by those who are more financially privileged, and therefore more able to help support the programs than those with limited means. We should also recognize that those who are wealthier may look at such payments as being onerous and burdensome. However, when one considers the alternative, not being able to support such programs and putting their very survival—and the survival of those who depend on them—in doubt, it's not difficult to imagine what might result. Is that acceptable to a country that was founded on the understanding that those more financially able *should* contribute more to assure our freedoms are maintained? If suddenly those more financially able choose to not cooperate and instead shirk their duty to support the Declaration of Independence and the Constitution, Bill of Rights, and all, our whole governmental structure will collapse and the basic tenets under which this country was founded will become null and void.

What a travesty it would be to let our whole democratic system collapse because there aren't enough patriots who love this country enough to make the small sacrifices necessary to assure that our freedoms remain secure. God help us if that should happen. We must always remember that living in America is indeed a privilege; it is nothing but good fortune to enjoy the bountiful benefits of all the many freedoms, including freedom from governmental interference, that living here provides most Americans. We should be willing to ensure that those less fortunate are able to enjoy some of the same benefits the rest enjoy daily. It is simply the right thing to do.

10. Issue ten has to do with **homeland security** and how we should deal with countries that pose a threat to the world and the United States by procuring nuclear devices or developing dangerous weapons. Should we continue to use a diplomatic or a military strategy to deal with such problems?

When the whole is considered—practicality, integrity, mind, and heart—compromise occurs and laws are passed.

In my next chapter, I will explain the steps that I believe must be taken to accomplish that goal of financial tranquility and political harmony that we so desire in our lives.

CHAPTER 9

WISE WORDS FROM WASHINGTON

S imply put, our politicians today must give up their self-centered
search for greater power, fame, and fortune as political goals. In their
place, they must substitute being other-centered, and through altruism,
empathy, and compassion, and because of love of country, *compromise*
with their fellow politicians so legislation gets passed that will benefit all
Americans.

Washington's "Farewell Address"

George Washington's Farewell Address was originally published in David
Claypool's *American Daily Advertiser* on September 19, 1796, under the
title "The Address of General Washington To The People of The United
States on his Declining of the Presidency of the United States." The title
was referring to Washington's refusal to take a third term in office, which
he would have easily won. Because of its instant popularity, it didn't take
long for the letter to be reprinted in newspapers across the country and later
be made into a pamphlet. Ultimately, the work was later named "Farewell
Address," as it was Washington's valedictory address representing his forty-
five years of service to America's new republic, first during the French and
Indian War, through the American Revolution, and finally, as the nation's
first president.

Because people in the 1700s spoke a much more formal variety of English, which I consider to be a beautiful means of speaking, and standard spellings did not exist until late in that century, it can be difficult at times to understand. I had to read Washington's "Farewell Address" several times to understand the essence of what he meant. Here is my interpretation with his words in quotation marks:

Washington urged his fellow Americans to recognize the "immense value" of their "national union" to their "collective and individual happiness." He urged his citizens to honor their attachment to one another and to their country. And to resist any attempts to destroy that bond. He stated that if this "immense value" was treated with respect and not abused, and if they were "cordial" and affable with one another, their nation's inherent beauty and potential would neither tarnish nor be tainted by neglect.

Empathy Is Important to All Our Lives

In order for politicians and nonpoliticians alike to do as Washington urges us all to do, it is for us all to periodically reflect on our lives, and through introspection, empathy, and, compassion begin to understand that it's the relationships we have with each other that provide the happiness we all desire in life. It's difficult *not* to follow the golden rule, "Do unto others as you would have them to do unto you," if you are preprogrammed to be empathetic and compassionate to every person you meet. It's very difficult *not* to treat someone with love and respect if you're able to see a little bit of yourself in that person.

People want to feel that their presence in your life makes a difference to you. You have to genuinely feel love for them and trust that they will show the same respect to you as you show them.

In order to be loving toward others, a certain amount of introspection or reflection is important to do periodically. Because knowing how you got to the point in your life that you're at, helps you better understand your reactions to others. You might not feel as open with somebody as you'd like to, or as free to show them that you care about them if they trigger something within you that signals "caution, tread lightly," or "careful, that person's not to be trusted." It can be instructive to know what or whom that person reminds you of.

It is only when you're able to reflect and understand your inner motivations that you begin to understand there's a third dimension to your whole existence that you may never have realized. This process teaches you how to be yourself without censure, judgment, or criticism from others. Knowing yourself helps you to also appear authentic and real in relationship to others. Because you are.

Being a politician in the way it's practiced today makes it very difficult to engage in self-reflection, whether to enrich your relationship with others or just yourself. That's most understandable; if you have a hidden agenda—which is to capture that person's vote—it is hard to be candid, authentic, and real with the voter.

It's also awfully hard to demonstrate unconditional love if you're a politician. That's because in the back of your head, you want something, therefore, you're going to tell people what they want to hear rather than how you really feel about the matter. It's only when the both of you are of the same political persuasion that you can genuinely be yourself. That's because then you'd both have the same cognitive style, so you feel comfortable with one another—you don't feel threatened by a view different from your own; your relationship with each other is free from cognitive dissonance.

Political extremism involves overly simplistic explanations for the country's problems and the belief that these problems result from the malevolence of one or more political members of the oppositional party. Those *evil-doers* are always named, whether by their party label, such as Republican or Democrat, or their individual names. Furthermore, the extremists believe that if the sinful opposing party member(s) would only listen to *the Truth*, with a capital T, all of the country's woes would be solved.

Political extremism encourages the extremist to pursue narrow policy paths without regard to nuance, consequences, or representation. That being so, more than a minority of our politicians and nonpoliticians alike engage in extremism.

Giving simple explanations for complex problems fosters extremism. For example, if you overgeneralize and offer one or a few all-inclusive beliefs to solve all of our country's problems, such as increase or cut taxes, reduce size of government, support corporate management, support the worker—you are engaging in extremism. One size doesn't fit all.

Ignorance and narrow-mindedness nurtures extremism, which in turn, feeds on itself, causing further ignorance, narrow-mindedness, and lack of knowledge. That kind of thinking hampers further discussion, which helps fosters prejudice and bias of views different than your own. *Narrow-mindedness and prejudice can foster ignorance and intolerance. Broad-mindedness and knowledge can foster acceptance and enlightenment.*

When political parties are polarized to the extent that compromise is not possible and where blind allegiance to party or ideology becomes the order of the day, our liberties, as spelled out in our Constitution, become jeopardized and threatened. Policy is no longer made as a result of vigorous discussion, but rather, is attained through clandestine and secret meetings.

Because political extremism prevents further inquiry and exploration of views different from your own, the search for political truth and enlightenment is not possible. If that were true here, that would sadden me, because you might not be willing to read this chapter and what I have to say about our country's Constitution; nor would you try to understand why I think we need to make a few long overdue repairs to that document in order to get this country moving in the right direction again.

Clearly, Washington foresaw the potential for dissension. He urged his country to be vigilant to any hostile forces from within or from without that may alienate any portion of our country from one another. Indeed, his final remarks were prompted in part by his reaction to the bitter dissention existing between Alexander Hamilton, who founded the Federalist Party, and Thomas Jefferson, who is credited for having founded the Democratic-Republican Party, originally called the Anti-Federalists Party. At the time, Jefferson was Washington's secretary of state, and Hamilton was his secretary of the treasury. The acrimony between the two men, and their cohorts, began during Washington's second term.

James Madison, who was initially a Federalist, became a Democratic-Republican and entered the political fray in support of Jefferson's vitriolic comments about Treasury Secretary Hamilton's handling of the country's financial matters. Even by the end of Washington's presidency, the potential for the nation's political future was becoming tarnished and besmirched. If the country didn't stay the course and work for the country's best interests rather than allow politics to destroy the country's integrity, it could fail.

The "Farewell Address" cautions the country to avoid the "baneful effects of the spirit of party" influences. My interpretation of what he said was that he feared the people's needs and wishes could be undermined by unsavory political leaders appealing to their voting public's passions and prejudices, rather than candidly stating the nation's needs and interests as they see them, free of demagogic rhetoric. He also stated that US diplomacy should "steer clear of permanent alliances." The country should "trust to temporary alliances for extraordinary emergencies," clearly for the same reasons.

Because Washington knew the danger of being identified with political parties and practices, he saw very little use for their existence, feeling they could easily become dissentious and factious. His concern was that they would dominate political thought at the expense of the people's wishes.

Unfortunately, because of cognitive dissonance, personal and party loyalty, and selfish interests, the politicians of yesteryear—as well as the politicians of today—heeded little of Washington's advice. In fact, with the exception of Washington's warning to avoid permanent military alliances with other nations, which didn't happen until after WWII, politicians have taken little note of any of Washington's warnings, though he continues to be the most admired and respected statesman in our history.

Not that the wisdom of any other president has been heeded either. One of the worst tendencies of our political system is that down through the years, in their state-of-the-union and farewell addresses, numerous presidents have warned Congress and the American citizens what kind of "the people's business" needed tending and what troublesome political trends should be avoided, yet party politics have trumped national interests and concerns time and again. At best, when there has been some kind of follow-through, like President Nixon urging Congress to work toward national energy independence, the response has turned out to be short-lived or partially but not completely attained.

For example, with the help of presidents Nixon, Ford, and Carter, our country established *strategic energy independence* in 1982. In spite of some failures, the energy policies enacted by these three presidents eventually succeeded, culminating less than ten years after the oil embargo. However, because other presidents failed to keep their eye on the ball and continue following through with previously established presidential policies, the price of oil has continued to plague our country's economic security and we have yet to become energy independent.

In order to fully understand what we're talking about, we must make a distinction between being *strategically* energy independent—like we were in 1982, when we had enough for emergencies—versus being *completely* energy independent because we have enough of the stuff so that we don't need to import oil from other countries under any circumstances.

It's hard to believe, but there were earlier times in our country's history when we were so oil-rich that we not only didn't need to have to depend on other countries to supply us with any oil whatsoever, but we had a surplus. That was prior to 1950. At that time, our country was producing over 50 percent of the world's oil. We had enough oil to supply our own needs and plenty for export as well.

What happened? After WWII, the economic explosion and expansion of industry and demand for vehicles in the USA created an oil demand in this country that our wells couldn't supply.

Even with the countries around the world developing their own wells and supply channels, the demand for the *liquid gold* far out-paced the supply available at any given time, thus causing the price of oil to rise when the demand for it increased. As big, developing nations are growing, like China and India, the demand will continue to increase, thus, ultimately causing the price of oil to continue to rise.

Furthermore, since the price of oil in the United States is based on government management (politically driven) and not due to production (supply and demand), the amount of federal taxes applied to each gallon of gas and governmental subsidies determines the cost.

116

Turmoil in any significant oil-producing nation—like the Middle East, North Africa, or Venezuela—can cause oil prices to rise. However, the price of gas in America continues to lag significantly behind Europe, where the Europeans pay at least double what Americans pay. Norway is one of the highest oil-paying countries. As of this writing, Oslo, Norway was paying the equivalent of $9.28 per gallon of gas. It's not because of lack of fossil fuel, because they have a thriving oil industry in the North Atlantic. Therefore, obviously the reason the price of oil is so high is due to other factors—taxes and subsidies and government policy.

Because of the immediate need of establishing a viable energy program—whether it's using alternate energy sources like natural gas, wind energy, electric energy, solar energy, nuclear energy, or some kind of energy source in the future that needs yet to be discovered—either private enterprise or government-sponsored programs need to be devised to deal with this most pressing problem.

Any ongoing *strategic energy-independence* program should be viewed as but a stopgap measure to achieve energy independence. That's because whatever the need to tap into that reserve might be, a permanent solution to achieve total energy independence for this nation is required, since need may exhaust supply at any given time. And then what do we do?

Whether it is a government- or private-enterprise-sponsored program, Americans will need to make whatever sacrifices necessary to make the program work. Our quality of life and survival as a nation is dependent upon the success of such a program.

Political parties as we know them today—with such technological enhancements as the telephone, Internet, frequent political meetings, unified platforms, and televised conventions—were nonexistent during Washington's time. He, his cabinet, and the other leaders of the day relied heavily on the written word, in the form of letters (missives), and verbal communication, in the form of discussions and debates, to communicate with one another.

Washington's warnings against the establishment of political parties becoming too influential in determining governmental policy continued to fall on deaf political ears over the life of our country. Instead of politicians making independent decisions based on what's best for *all* Americans, political parties have crystallized their power and become stronger and stronger. So too has their clout to ensure that legislative decisions are based on political affiliation rather than individual and national needs and goals.

According to Ron Chernow in his book *Washington,* in one of Washington's letters, he stated that he felt the Constitution had brought forth "a government of the people: that is to say, a government in which all power is derived from, and at stated periods reverts to, them—and that, in its operation … is purely a government of laws made and executed by the fair substitutes of the people alone."[51]

The key operative words in that statement are "executed by the fair substitutes of the people alone," which simply means the *elected officials,* who represent the people should be fair, hence unbiased and unprejudiced for or against the people they serve. It's difficult to believe that's being done when today's politicians appear more beholden to their political parties rather than to *all* the people they are elected to serve.

Political parties weren't as powerful in influencing politicians in the 1700s as they are today. For one, they didn't really get established officially until approximately ten years after Washington became president. The enhancement of news coverage may be part of the reason for that as well. Politicians certainly did not get the media attention they get today. However, that doesn't excuse politicians from abusing their Congressional offices for political gain at the expense of the people they have sworn to serve and protect.

The political vilification and defamation that Washington experienced during the last term of his presidency and his stern warnings against partisanship would be examples of the first two of the Four Foundations of Freedom (private and public virtues) to which the Founding Father referred. (See chapter 5 for a fuller explanation.)

Although Thomas Jefferson's thinking was initially consonant with President Washington's, as Washington's second term progressed, Jefferson

---

[51] Chernow, p. 565.

began to express great consternation over Secretary of Treasury Alexander Hamilton's excessive manipulation of Washington's monetary policy. As Federalists, Hamilton and Washington believed in the importance of a strong central bank, fashioned after England's, and a strong central government. They felt that a comprehensive economic and fiscal program would secure the country's (government) financial and economic health and stability.

Meanwhile, Thomas Jefferson and James Madison favored a decentralized and smaller banking system, realizing that such a structure would better accommodate itself to an agricultural economy—which they believed would be more inherently productive than a manufacturing economy. It was easier to see the potential for agriculture to flourish at that time rather than manufacturing, since industrialization had not yet occurred. But beyond that, the two statesmen did not trust, in the political arena, that industrialists (manufacturers) would as readily exhibit the first two foundations of freedom (those private and public virtues) as they believed landholders (farmers) were capable of showing.

We must remember America had just won a long and costly war, both in human lives lost and debt incurred. The government was millions of dollars in debt. The paper currency issued by the Continental Congress had decreased to near worthlessness. The states, not the federal government, all issued their own currency. Combined with the foreign currencies also circulating, this fiscal diversity caused much confusion over the value of money. Additionally, there was rising unemployment since the war, and the government's bonds were trading at a fraction of their face value.

As discussed earlier, Shay's Rebellion was symptomatic of the financial ill health that the young nation, the United States of America, was experiencing in the aftermath of the Revolutionary War. There had been a real need to establish a federal government that could exert monetary control over the thirteen quasi-independent state governments.

Thomas Jefferson and James Madison, the "Anti-Federalists," were fearful that the federal government would become *too influential* in dictating policy and that if allowed too much power, the president would eventually become a monarch. To prevent that from happening, they believed the smaller the federal government the better, and that there should not be too much power invested in any cabinet position and most certainly not the presidency.

Washington had similar concerns. Early on, he had no interest in maintaining any semblance of power and, for that reason, had resigned his commission at the end of the Revolutionary War. Similarly, one reason he did not want to serve a third term as president was that he was fearful of the office becoming too much like a monarchy.

There were indeed officers of the army who wanted Washington to become king of the new nation, but he rejected that kind of thinking, reminding them that that was one of the reasons the war was fought: to prevent another monarchy from being established. Washington believed that the leadership of our young country should be determined by popular vote, not determined by birthright.

Although seeds of political distrust and bickering were first planted during Washington's time, institutionalized polarization didn't really take root as the heart of congressional thought and legislation until politicians *began to run for the 2012 presidential election.* Certainly, we've had dark periods in American history down through the ages—to mention a few (in no particular order): such periods as HUAC (House Un-American Activities Committee) in the 1950s during and after the so-called McCarthy Red Scare period, when the right wing frightened Americans into believing that the Communists were going to take over the United States (whatever that meant); the period after Lincoln's assassination during the Restoration period, also known as the Carpetbagger era, after the Civil War; and the Vietnam era, where both the Democrats and the Republicans were on one side, and the people were on the other ... I could go on, but I'll stop here.

However, what has been different about the polarization today is the width and breadth of the division—there are more numbers that represent each side of the schism. If you identify your political leanings as being either Democratic or Republican and wish to rigidly support the party line and not split your vote, you are inclined to indiscriminately vote

Republican or Democratic, depending on your prejudices and inherent biases, as reflected in your allegiance to your party politics.

What makes today's two political sides so menacing and ominous is the power that both parties wield. The question is no longer what are the voting issues that should be considered, but rather what party should I embrace, and therefore, will support with my vote. That's why I feel each political party has hijacked our government. It's no longer a government by and for the people, but rather, a government by and for the political parties.

That's when legislative decisions appeared to be based more on party affiliation than on what was best for *all* the people, which includes a country diverse in age, class, and ethnicity, with two sexes and at least two sexual orientations. As a result, in most cases, little legislation got passed because *neither party wished to compromise* sufficiently for that to occur. This pernicious and toxic political environment has increased in greater degrees from one year to the next, starting at the beginning of the twenty-first century to the present.

The Revolutionary and Civil Wars and the events leading up to the First and Second World Wars were events in American history that forced Americans to think about their values and beliefs in ways that daily life today does not require. Because the citizens of our nation aren't faced with a monumental crisis on the scale of the four great wars, the kinds of abuses of our basic values and standards as a nation are much more insidious and subtle. Because there isn't that kind of urgency to reflect on our individual integrity in the same way we needed to do during those crises, we have allowed the political climate of the day to pretty much direct our thinking. Because of our mental laziness, we have allowed the media and politicians to determine what we should think and believe—resulting in a consumer and entertainment mentality replacing critical thinking.

Let's return to the early 1950s to understand the regressive steps we as a nation began to take that have caused many of our country's politicians to exploit our nation's integrity for their own personal gain.

CHAPTER 10

WE ARE ALL PRODUCTS OF OUR TIME

After World War II, because of pent-up needs, the demand for goods and services grew at breakneck speed. As a result, employment opportunities went through the roof, providing jobs for the service men returning home from the war. This was not true for women, however. In fact, whether they liked it or not, most of the women working for the war effort were either laid off or fired when the men returned. They were forced to leave the workforce in record numbers. As a result, many of the women were never able to enjoy the money and independence their own jobs had given them when they did their patriotic duty working in defense plants and doing the same kinds of jobs their male counterparts would have done if they weren't overseas fighting the enemy. Similarly, black workers came back to less freedom and opportunity than they'd been fighting for during the war. This is how seeds of discontent are sown.

However, with the advent of the GI Bill, our nation felt flush and magnanimous after victories in Europe and the Pacific. There was good reason to feel that way. It is generally believed that WWII helped end the Great Depression. In part, that was because the war gave Americans thousands, if not millions, of jobs. For example, men too old to serve in the military worked in factories. Women worked in factories alongside them—building airplanes, ships, tanks, and other supplies to help in the war effort. By mobilizing the unemployed, we aided our economy. This scenario was in sharp contrast to what existed before the war when women weren't expected to work outside the house and if they did, there were only limited professions available to them—like nursing, teaching, and secretarial jobs.

The reason most of the women who worked to support the war effort were unable to continue a similar kind of employment during a peacetime economy was because a powerful chauvinistic propaganda machine quickly emerged that stated "a woman's place is in the home." As a result of that myth, women who worked in defense plants during the war abruptly left the labor force after the war was won. Along with their wartime jobs, they lost years of status and position in the late '40s, not to be regained until the 1970s.

The dominant jobs available to women who returned to peacetime employment were nurses, secretaries, and teachers. Don't misunderstand me, I'm not suggesting that those kinds of jobs' intrinsic worth and value were inferior or less ego-enhancing, for either sex, than another job might be. What I am suggesting is that if, after the war, a woman would rather be able to do a job similar to what she had done when she worked in a defense plant, such an opportunity would likely not be available to her in the same way it would be for her male counterpart.

A companion myth equally destructive to women's sense of autonomy and self-image was the "father knows best" catchphrase. Like the other fairy tale, it too had a life of its own, for it wasn't until about the 1970s when society began to seriously question the credibility of such thinking.

For men, that belief that "father knows best" was just as insidious a slogan as the other one, "a woman's place is in the home," because it encouraged dogmatic thinking and all the destructive behavior that bigoted belief breeds—which, to this day, continues to fan the flames of conflict between the sexes.

I lived under the *father knows best* myth throughout my developmental years and twenty years into my marriage. So it had a long time to adversely affect not only my life, but my family's lives as well.

Because I had lived with that myth for so long, I *believed* it to be true, never mind how destructive that false truth was to my wife and children. But my viewing myself that way caused harm to both my own self-image—because of course I did not always know best—and that of my wife, my son, and my twin daughters' self-images as well.

So, my whole family, including myself, suffered from two myths that impacted how we looked at ourselves and each other. By the time the two fairy tales no longer haunted our psyches, my children were about ten or so years old; they had been exposed to that kind of malignant thinking throughout the most critical years of their development. This is the damage cognitive dissonance can wreak on a personal level. Expand this to the relationship of citizens in a nation and we come to where we are now.

Obviously, being exposed to such thinking impacts our lives differently from person to person. If the exposure is long and other people in the family believe the garbage—whether it's the father or the mother—which parent holds most of the family power and is most influential in the family constellation will have an impact on what and how firm such malignant beliefs are held by family members.

Many male chauvinists who are part of our society may wish to perpetuate those two malevolent myths to their own exploitative advantage, which is self-aggrandizement or personal gain at someone's else's expense—usually all the females, but even the males in our society. I say males, because by identifying with the dominator, the male who's modeling his behavior after that kind of person simply perpetuates and expands the thinking that subjugating others is a good thing to others in our society. In fact, unwittingly, that kind of thinking may become part of a person's political thinking. When that happens, because of cognitive dissonance, it begins to have a mind of its own in that the person who holds such a belief begins to look for evidence to further support his belief system and ignore points of view contrary to his or her thinking. That's when a person not only doesn't accept what's said, but doesn't even hear that contrary points of view exist.

We must remember that during the time of our Founding Fathers, the major industry was farming—and governmental policy was, in part, formulated with that thought in mind. A hundred seventy years later, the Second World War ending signaled the time when our economic base dramatically shifted away from mostly farming jobs to mostly manufacturing jobs and services. This tendency away from the rural economy continues even to this day, as we now move from a mostly manufacturing economy to a mostly service economy.

Although Europe was devastated by the war, our country emerged more powerful, both militarily and economically, than ever before.

Our country's leaders could literally feel generous toward the countries that were our allies and merciful toward those who we defeated during that great wars. The United States enacted the European Recovery Plan in 1947 to rebuild Europe after World War II. Known as the Marshal Plan, it was named for its sponsor, General George Marshal, who was secretary of state at the time. The reason for the plan was twofold: to help the war-torn European countries recover from the devastation of war and to prevent Communism from gaining a stronghold in those countries

Some countries received little aid, and some countries, like Japan and the USSR, refused any aid whatsoever. However, US allies Austria, Belgium, Denmark, Greece, Iceland, the Netherlands, Norway, Portugal, Sweden, Switzerland, and Turkey all received funds for reconstruction. Even our former enemy partition, West Germany, and Italy, who was part of the Axis forces, received Marshal Plan aid.

In 1951, the Marshall Plan was terminated, which coincided with the United States becoming involved in the Korean Conflict. Since there were fewer funds allocated by the US Congress to European recovery at that time, the plan was ended.

In total, the US government spent $13.3 billion (USD), from 1948–1951, on this program—or a whopping $120 billion in 2012 dollars.

The plan succeeded in helping to restore some European economies by helping them increase productivity, thereby stimulating economic growth and promoting trade—all of which improved the participating countries' standard of living and strengthened their economic, social, and political structures. Although the Marshall Plan could not stem the takeover of Communism in certain countries, it did help to contribute to the containment of the spread of Communism in others.

The termination of the Marshall Plan and the advent of the Korean War signaled the *symbolic* termination of our country's selfless and giving spirit and our willingness to work toward something greater than ourselves—namely to help other nations in need.

Charitable giving soon stopped being our citizenry's modus operandi. It was replaced by the mantra, quid pro quo: this for that, something for something, that which a party receives (or is promised) in return for something given or promised. That type of transaction or implied agreement has nothing to do with unconditionally responding to the needs of other nations. Rather than have the rational side of our thinking work in conjunction with the empathetic side to allow our integrity *some* expression, the implied quid pro quo agreement became a political transaction where scheming and conniving became the order of the day, in hopes our country would be better able to secure itself against enemy attack or that the oil-rich nations would help supply our nation's energy needs.

Nowadays, how other countries react to us is almost exclusively determined by our nation's financial worth, expressed in foreign aid, rather than the individual and collective value our politicians place on our nation's integrity. When that attitude prevails, our willingness to form alliances with other countries begins to be based on how much security and/or economic benefit could be derived from forming such a coalition. That's all done pretty much void of following our collective integrity, as represented by our nation's proverbial soul, where we let our country's archetypal heart dictate the kinds of actions we show to other nations by providing humane aid to countries in need.

As soon as the national agreements we make with other countries involves financial or military aid in exchange for goods and services, it becomes a political transaction. We, as a nation, then become more concerned about winning favor or retaining power than maintaining principles. It's then easy to see how our nation's integrity quickly erodes. That's because what we no longer value within us is our ability to appreciate each other's integrity or honesty, or related qualities such as transparency, authenticity, empathy, and compassion that demonstrate our caring for one another and why we're proud to be Americans. However, in order to have those qualities become manifest, our nation's politicians must elevate their politics to a higher level, as Lincoln or Washington did, and so act as statesmen and stateswomen rather than sacrifice our integrity for political gain.

Not that we were in a position to continue to give to needy nations in the same way, or even at all, after the Korean War took place. What I do take issue with is how we have used our foreign aid since then. It has too often been in an effort to buy the support and friendship of other nations, some of whom have governments antithetical to our own, and therefore, whose loyalty and assurance that they would come to our aid in time of need is suspect. Or they may be helping us eliminate terrorism on the one hand but on the other providing safe havens for Al Qaeda, as is the case with Pakistan.

Since I'm not a foreign policy expert, I'll refrain from passing judgment on those kinds of issues, however, in our effort to maintain peace, we have neglected the needs of many American citizens, who, through no fault of their own, are struggling just to eke out a living from one day to the next.

If our elected politicians viewed today's situation in a similar way that those who fought in the Revolutionary War or the Civil War, WWI, or WWII viewed their country, today's politicians would have reprioritized how their foreign aid should be distributed. They certainly would have been more responsive to the human needs that many American citizens are struggling with in their own country today.

If we are the richest nation on earth, don't you think it should mean something to be an American citizen? No American should go without adequate shelter, medical care, or three squares a day. It has nothing to do with entitlement, socialism, being a Republican or a Democrat or an independent; it has everything to do with what it means to be an American and what was once the "American way": *It should be done because it's the* RIGHT *thing to do.*

To provide for those who can't provide for themselves does assume that they have done everything possible to *pull themselves up by their own bootstraps* and to better their quality of life but because of circumstances beyond their control are unable to do so.

A vast number of people in the labor force have been laid off for six months, two years, or more. It's fair to assume that a lot of those who are currently unemployed have done everything in their power to become employed again and hopefully will be able to become *gainfully* employed in the not-too-distant future. Because they have the wherewithal to improve their lot in life on their own when economic conditions for the country improve, the government is not expected to provide adequate food, housing, or medical care for people who are able-bodied in mind, spirit, and physicality and are quite able to hold down a job that is appropriate to their age, sex, and life experience.

I believe that, tragically, what has taken place is that our culture has switched from valuing our community and relationships to placing an undue significance on money and material possessions as a means to attain happiness and self-worth. So we make outcasts of those who are struggling, judging them as worthless and not wanting that worthlessness to rub off on us.

If our country's politicians had more of the mental set that was present during the four great wars, they would have been more willing to allow the government to respond to the bona fide needs of their fellow Americans—or those citizens who, chronically, and through no fault of their own, find it impossible to properly provide for themselves. In order to do that, today's citizenry would need strong political leaders who would clarify the issues and set the examples. They could do that by responding to the legitimate needs of others by passing legislation to help those in need, regardless of party affiliation, and urging their fellow Americans to develop the mind-set to be generous of heart and spirit, to compassionately support governmental programs that help our fellow Americans who have genuine chronic needs of a basic nature. It is through words *and* actions that leaders show their voting constituents what this country should be all about.

Of course we all know obtaining all kinds of wealth does not automatically assure happiness or ascribe worth. That's because what is left wanting, remaining dormant and starving for expression, is the part of our personalities that makes us feel whole and undivided, and therefore authentic. *That is our integrity.* Because of lack of use, that part of our being that makes life worth living, ultimately, becomes arid and barren.

In order to help it become fertile and vibrant again—where we would feel revitalized enough to restore our unconditional other-centeredness and perform acts of kindness—the first order of the day is to stop pointing our fingers at others and to work on getting our own house in order. We do that by deciding what's important in our lives. The choice is whether to feed our avaricious appetites by acquiring more material goods to fill the emptiness in our lives, or to respond to the needs of people besides ourselves. Or we could simply help others, and in that way respect their and our integrity. Then maybe we would feel good about ourselves and what we're about again.

When politicians seek celebrity or power as the motivation for seeking political office, rather than seeking to serve their beloved country and their fellow human beings, they obviously are no better off than the ordinary citizen who robotically works to obtain wealth alone, believing it will assure their happiness.

Absolute Power

The origin of the saying "Power corrupts; absolute power corrupts absolutely" is a man called John Emerich Edward Dalberg Acton, the first Baron Acton (1834–1902). A Catholic historian and moralist, Lord Acton expressed this opinion in a letter to Church of England Bishop Mandell Creighton in 1887: "Power tends to corrupt, and absolute power corrupts absolutely. Great men are almost always bad men."

Applying that saying in the world of modern politics, here, in the twenty-first century, it can be rephrased by saying the more power we grant to our elected officials, the more corrupt they seem to become. The reason there's more truth to that saying than we'd like to believe is because political power is like fame and fortune, it becomes so addictive that politicians who are under its spell can't get enough of it.

Political scientists define power as "the ability to influence the behavior of others with or without resistance."[52] In the case of the American citizen, whether or not the power that is used by politicians is corrupt or not

---

[52] *Wikipedia*, "Power (Philosophy)," http://en.wikipedia.org/wiki/Power_(philosophy).

is determined by whether such power is used to satisfy the politician's own personal needs or to serve the needs of the American citizenry the politician was elected to serve.

The more power politicians have, the more likely corruption occurs, because they begin to become addicted to the money and prestige that their office brings to them. It is then that they begin to become duplicitous and self-serving.

ABC News writer Chris Cuomo took issue with such prestige in November 2011:

> For all the talk from those in Congress about how we all have to tighten our belts and make do with what we have, you would expect your lawmakers to follow suit … But this is a case of actions speaking louder than words.[53]

Cuomo observed that a twenty-year member of Congress of at least sixty-two years of age collects a lifelong pension of more than $50,000 a year. Meanwhile, employees in the private sector who qualify for a pension receive $16,000 per year on average.

As Cuomo noted, Congress "has a better pension plan than just about anybody."

Even a dead congressman or congresswoman can make plenty of money—as reported by *Fox News,* the family of the late West Virginia Senator Robert Byrd would be paid his salary the next year—all $193,000 of it.[54]

In the House, *Fox News* reported, representatives can spend more than $900,000 on salaries for as many as eighteen permanent employees, not to mention about $250,000 for travel and other expenses, like office supplies. That's a lot of staplers.

---

[53] http://abcnews.go.com/US/chris-cuomos-give-break-Congressional-perks/ story?id=14884393#.T4I_-ppAZsw.

[54] http://www.foxnews.com/politics/2010/09/29/benefits-members-Congress-shabby/.

Senators get even bigger allowances—in 2010, the average allocation topped $3.3 million. Meanwhile, the article noted, "the work week lately has been relatively sparse … the Senate has averaged about three working days on Capitol Hill."

The greed and hunger for power fostered by these perks can damage politicians' integrity.

With power comes arrogance. In order for politicians to justify maintaining their self-serving stances, they then begin to convince themselves that the American people do not know how to govern themselves, a view that Washington would adamantly deny.

An example of power addiction is when newly elected Congressional candidates swear that they will only serve one term if elected. However, as their first term is soon to expire, invariably, it seems, they suddenly say they wish to run another term. The reasons candidates put forward for this kind of behavior might be called *rationalization*, which is simply providing a plausible but not the real reason for behaving as they do. The real reason they suddenly have a change of heart is that they have become inebriated with the perks that come with the job. Not only is the power and prestige intoxicating, but also the generous financial remuneration in the form of salary and the lucrative lifetime pension benefits they receive. These can become very compelling reasons to maintain the status quo. In order to prevent this self-aggrandizement from continuing, I will offer some specific recommendations in the next chapter.

If our Founding Fathers could observe firsthand what has happened to our beloved nation over the two-hundred-plus years since we became the United States of America, I am sure they would agree with the following proposed changes that reflect the spirit and intent of what they said when they framed the Constitution. The few changes would take the form of amendments.

CHAPTER 11

FIXING OUR CONSTITUTION

As political needs change over time, the Constitution is designed to accommodate modification should repairs be needed. The mechanism for repairing the Constitution so that the freedoms and rights of the American citizenry are preserved is through Congress and the amendment process. Amendments throughout the history of the United States reflect changes that were required as the country's political needs changed and our citizens' views evolved. We discussed this at length in chapter 3 in the section "The Bill of Rights," which were the first ten amendments passed before the Constitution was even ratified.

This chapter proposes how to fix our Constitution for our time—which is to have Congress pass specific amendments to hold our elected officials to their responsibility to respond to the needs of *all* Americans and not just those who are best positioned to serve the *politicians'* needs and desires.

Some lobbyists, for example, have corrupted the government with their tactics. One of the more notorious lobbyists, Jack Abramoff, "became a master at showering gifts on lawmakers in return for their votes on legislation and tax breaks favorable to his clients [in the 1980s and '90s]. He was so good at it, he took home $20 million a year," according to CBS News.[55]

---

55 http://www.cbsnews.com/8301-18560_162-57319075/jack-abramoff-the-lobbyists-playbook/.

It's worth noting that Abramoff ultimately went to jail for his practices, but before that happened, he spent years influencing politicians with lavish gifts, including access to private jets and luxurious golf outings. He offered free meals at an upscale restaurant he owned, along with tickets to sporting events—a million dollars' worth annually.

His best tactic, Abramoff acknowledges, was simply to bribe Congressional staffers with future jobs that would pay triple the employee's current salary.

"When we would become friendly with an office and they were important to us, and the chief of staff was a competent person, I would say … 'You know, when you're done working on the Hill, we'd very much like you to consider coming to work for us.' Now the moment I said that to them or any of our staff said that to 'em, that was it. We owned them."[56]

Abramoff described himself as having "very strong influence in a hundred [Congressional] offices at the time … In those days, I would view that as a failure. Because that leaves 335 offices that we didn't have strong influence in."

The *Washington Post* described him as "an ingenious dealmaker who hatched interlocking schemes that exploited the machinery of government and trampled the norms of doing business in Washington."[57]

What do any of Abramoff's efforts have to do with legislation? It's hard to imagine Abraham Lincoln or Thomas Jefferson having a flattering answer to that question. It's time to protect America from the selfishness of politicians.

I would imagine that many readers of this treatise assume that it would take ever-and-a-day to get a constitutional amendment ratified by the states. History demonstrates that is not always so. If the American citizens want amendments to be ratified, they are able to accelerate the process. That's called "people power."

Of the twenty-seven amendments to the Constitution, seven took one year or less to become the law of the land—all because of public pressure.

---

56 Ibid.
57 http://www.washingtonpost.com/wp-dyn/content/article/2005/12/28/AR2005122801588.html.

The Twenty-Sixth Amendment, which ensures the vote to all citizens over the age of eighteen, was proposed on March 23, 1971, and ratified in a hundred days. The reason for the speed of the ratification was that the people demanded it. The ratification represented the will of the people. Remember, that was before computers, e-mail, cell phones or any other high-tech personal communication devices that we have today were available.

Specific Amendment Recommendations

• **Term Limits:** One six-year term for our president, one six-year Senate term, and one six-year House term (435 members in the House and 100 members in the Senate = 535 congressional members). Note: the members of the House of Representatives should return home after they serve one six-year term, rather than three two-year terms.

Rationale: Serving as president and in Congress is an honor, not a career. The Founding Fathers envisioned *the citizen-statesmen* serving their country as president and Congresspersons for a brief period of time to help *the People* and then to go home to their businesses or plantations, leaving their government job to new people. They never foresaw working for the government as being a profession unto itself.

This is precisely what Republican Senator Tom Coburn of Oklahoma did. He pledged to serve in the House of Representatives for his allotted term limit of three two-year terms, and after six years in the House, chose not to run for his House seat again. During his hiatus from serving in government, he wrote a book about his Washington experience and titled it *Breach of Trust*. In 2010, he ran for the Senate and won. He promised to serve but one six-year term, finishing it in 2016. This has given him license to follow his own way, devoid of political allegiance to either party, much to the chagrin of both sides of the aisle.

When the Constitution and Bill of Rights were written, the framers, who were also members of the Second Continental Congress, made up of trades people, farmers, and lawyers, were mostly people of means and of some social standing. Regardless of their wealth, societal positions, and occupations, or how very diverse their backgrounds were, they were interested in writing the Constitution to reflect the needs of the *common man.* Considering their varied backgrounds and diverse socioeconomic levels, the fact they were able to come to a common agreement as to what should be put in the Constitution demonstrates that they were willing to forgo their selfish interests for the greater good (public virtue), which was accomplished through the political art of compromise.

To emphasize the importance of realizing the Constitution was written for the common man, in the last line of Lincoln's Gettysburg Address, he said, "And that government *of the people, by the people, for the people* [emphasis mine], shall not perish from the earth." That line alone suggests that the Constitution and Bill of Rights were written *of, by, and for* the people of the United States.

Another reason I favor term limits is that the president and members of Congress begin campaigning for their next term as soon as they enter their office building. If in the back of their minds, getting reelected is of paramount importance, it's very difficult to concentrate on current matters at hand and, at the same time, be true to oneself and the electorate. What suffers when that happens? You guessed it, their integrity.

Many politicians argue *against* term limits because the newly elected require so much time to learn the job. By the time they know what they're doing, there's not enough time left to get enough done to make it worth it.

My answer is to have the incumbent politician act as a tutor for the newly elected office holder until he or she has learned the job satisfactorily. How long the learning period needs to be would be determined over time. Because the president would also be required to serve only one term, the prior president would similarly shepherd the newly elected one along until he or she is reasonably comfortable with the job at hand. Both the newly elected politician and the incumbent would be paid the salary they would be due if either one was working that elected office independently.

Obviously, if any kind of a modification is required, an amendment addressing the problem would have to be passed.

Of course, regarding the Senate and the presidency, if, occasionally, more time than the average is required to learn the job, the incumbent can stay with the newly elected office holder for as long as necessary to develop the required level of competency to handle the office responsibilities. It is assumed that the retired Congressperson or president would be more than willing to do that, since I would assume he or she would see serving in government as an *honor and a privilege.*

By having the incumbent work side by side with the newly elected president, or Congressperson, it would encourage bipartisanship, particularly in the case where one is a Republican and the other a Democrat. Nevertheless, regardless of the political makeup of the changing of the guard, what is encouraged is mutuality of objectives and a spirit of cooperation, as well as encouraging both politicians to work for something greater than themselves—*which is to be responsive to the needs of all Americans.*

I know that many, particularly the active, office-holding politicians, are going to vigorously object to my term-limits suggestion. Before they protest, however, they should ask themselves how they see themselves serving this nation. Is serving this nation like being a corporate executive who's running a company, primarily concerned with the bottom line and the profits the company makes? Or is it like being a civil servant who wants to preserve the liberty and way of life not only for themselves, but for all Americans?

If politicians really see serving their country as an honor and a privilege, then I would think there would be no contest as to the president and Congress being willing to leave office.

- **An Upper-Age Limit of House and Senate Members Should Be Established**

Rationale: There are times in each of our lives when we are not as sharp as we once were. The time Congress members should be allowed to serve is until they reach their seventy-fifth birthday. If they're going to reach that age while still in office, they shouldn't be allowed to run.

According to a report published on the website of the National Center for Biotechnology Information,

> Older adults exhibit significant deficits … Although the mechanisms underlying these age-related deficits are as yet poorly understood, the effects of such deficits are very likely far-reaching. Many complex everyday tasks such as decision making, problem

solving, and the planning of goal-directed behaviors require the integration and reorganization from a variety of sources. It seems likely that attention, speed of information processing, and the ability to inhibit irrelevant information are all important functions for effective performance of these higher-level cognitive tasks.[58]

"Decision making" and "problem solving" are two skill areas in which our politicians cannot afford to be lacking.

- **Supreme Court Judges Should Not Be Appointed for Life**

Rationale: The reason Supreme Court justices should *not* be appointed for life is the same reason Congressional members shouldn't be allowed to serve after they reach their seventy-fifth birthday. That's because their mental agility becomes less than optimum after that age. The time for judges to retire is after they reach their seventy-fifth birthday.

- **No Tenure/No Pension**

Rationale: US congressional salaries and benefits have been the source of taxpayer unhappiness and mythology over the years. Here are some facts for your consideration:

With respect to the rank-and-file members, the amount of the pension members of Congress receive depends on their years of service and the average of the highest three years of salary. By law, the starting amount of a member's retirement annuity may not exceed 80 percent of his or her final salary.

The current salary (2011) for rank-and-file members of the House and Senate is $174,000 per year.

Leaders of the House and Senate are paid a higher salary than rank-and-file members, of course. In the Senate: the party leaders of both majority and minority parties receive $193,400. In the House: the Speaker of the House receives $223,500, while the majority and minority leaders of the House each receive $193,400.

In 2006, the *average annual pension* for retired senators and representatives under the Civil Service Retirement System (CSRS) was

---

58 http://www.ncbi.nlm.nih.gov/books/NBK3885/.

$60,972, while ordinary government employees, who retire under the Federal Retirement Systems (FERS) or in combination with CSRS, received an average of only $25,952.

For the last several years, Congress has chosen to not increase their annual salary based on their legislated annual cost-of-living increase. In addition, individual members are free to turn down pay increases and some do choose to do so.

In order to help get our nation going in the right track, I believe it would be a good idea to publicize those members of Congress who turned down pay increases or even those who chose not to be paid for services rendered. There are indeed a number of politicians who are well-heeled enough and could most certainly do what General Washington did when he commanded his Continental Army—he refused receiving a salary throughout the war.

The First US Congress voted to pay Washington a salary of $25,000 a year—a large sum in 1789. Washington, already wealthy, declined the salary, since he valued his image as a selfless public servant. At Congress's urging, however, he ultimately accepted the payment. This too had a public-service motive. It was done to avoid setting a precedent whereby the presidency would be perceived as limited only to independently wealthy individuals who could serve without any salary.

Here in the twenty-first century, Tom Murse, contributing writer for About.com, reports on 2010 figures:

> Overall, members of Congress saw their personal wealth grow by more than 16 percent during the worst economic downturn in the United States since the Great Depression, according to financial disclosures submitted by lawmakers ...
>
> The median personal wealth for members of Congress grew to $911,500 in 2009, up from $785,515 in 2008, according to Center for Responsive Politics. Nearly half of the members of Congress are millionaires.
>
> Of the 261 millionaire members of Congress, fifty-five have an average calculated wealth of $10 million or more. [Jay] Rockefeller

and several other members of Congress reported personal wealth in the $100 million plus range.[59]

Dave Levinthal, writing for the Center for Responsive Politics (OpenSecrets.org), reports the following:

> WASHINGTON—Members of Congress are enjoying their own financial stimulus. "Despite a stubbornly sour national economy Congressional members' personal wealth collectively increased by more than 16 percent between 2008 and 2009," according to a new study by the Center for Responsive Politics of federal financial disclosures released earlier this year. And while some members' financial portfolios lost value, no need to bemoan most lawmakers' financial lot: Nearly half of them—261—are millionaires, a slight increase from the previous year, the Center's study finds. That compares to about 1 percent of Americans who lay claim to the same lofty fiscal status.
>
> And of these Congressional millionaires, fifty-five have an average calculated wealth in 2009 of $10 million or more, with eight in the $100 million-plus range.
>
> "Few federal lawmakers must grapple with the financial ills—unemployment, loss of housing, wiped out savings—that have befallen millions of Americans," said Sheila Krumholz, the Center for Responsive Politics' executive director. "Congressional representatives on balance rank among the wealthiest of wealthy Americans and boast financial portfolios that are all but unattainable for most of their constituents."[60]
>
> In 2009, the median wealth of a US House member stood at $765,010, up from $645,503 in 2008. The median wealth of a

---

59 Tom Murse, "Wealthiest Members of Congress," About.com, http://usgovinfo. about.com/od/usCongress/ss/Wealthiest-Members-of-Congress_3.htm.
60 Levinthal, Dave. "Congressional Members' Personal Wealth Expands Despite Sour National Economy." Opensecrets.org. 17 Nov. 2010. http://www.opensecrets. org/news/2010/11/congressional-members-personal-weal.html (20 Sept. 2011).

US senator was nearly $2.38 million, up from $2.27 million in 2008.

For all members of Congress regardless of chamber, median wealth in 2009 reached $911,510, up from $785,515 in 2008. This spike in personal wealth represents a notable rebound from the period between 2007 and 2008, when overall Congressional wealth slipped by more than 5 percent. Federal lawmakers' personal wealth climaxed in 2007—the pinnacle of nearly a decade's worth of steady asset value expansion.

History suggests that in addition to Benjamin Franklin, who very much saw serving as president and serving in Congress as being an honor, *not* a career, the Founding Fathers also envisioned the president and citizen legislators serving their term(s), and then returning home.

- **Campaign-Finance Reform**

Rationale: The amount of money necessary to run a campaign has gotten completely out of hand. Today, the only people who can run for president or even Congress, are those who are wealthy. The common man or woman with limited means is excluded from participating in the "We the People" government.

The Center for Responsive Politics (OpenSecrets.org) cites the following statistics on their table regarding the cost of campaigns (used by permission).

Historical Elections: The Money behind the Elections

Cycle *	Total Cost of Election	To Dems	To Repubs	Dem %	Repub %
2010	$3,648,232,683	$1,816,201,141	$1,772,688,000	50%	49%
2008*	$5,285,680,883	$3,006,088,428	$2,239,412,570	57%	42%
2006	$2,852,658,140	$1,360,120,917	$1,444,816,900	48%	51%
2004*	$4,147,304,003	$2,146,861,774	$1,963,417,015	52%	47%

2002	$2,181,682,066	$977,041,618	$1,183,255,932	45%	54%
2000*	$3,082,340,937	$1,311,910,043	$1,662,298,674	43%	54%
1998	$1,618,936,265	$731,878,353	$878,130,297	45%	54%

*Presidential election cycle

In today's political world, there is most certainly a need for public financing of elections, since the little guy—the person with limited financial means—can't even dream of running for Congress or most certainly president of the United States. Since the average cost of running and winning a seat in the US Congress, either in the House of Representatives or the Senate, runs more than one million dollars here in the twenty-first century, in order for you to make yourself a viable candidate, you need to provide a little *seed money* to establish yourself as a viable candidate and then hope your political party will help financially nurture your candidacy to political victory.

However, in 2009, the Supreme Court ruled 5–4 that free-speech rights, as expressed in the First Amendment of the United States Constitution, permits groups like corporations and labor unions to directly spend money on political campaigns. This allows special-interest money to unduly influence American politics, which will obviously diminish the influence of individual Americans who give small donations. Instead of the American voter influencing political futures, it's the politicians with the big bucks who receive the financial backing from corporations, unions, religious organizations, and/or individual wealthy donors and win the elections. This is a perfect example of how money *talks,* both from a literal and figurative standpoint.

Solution: To eliminate all of the thorny problems inherent in fairly and equitably managing campaign-finance donations—whether from corporations, groups of individuals, organized labor, or individual donors—one set of rules should apply to all those donating monies to individual political candidates. Congress should pass and the president sign a law allowing *only* individuals to make political contributions. The amount should be limited to three dollars as currently stated on each taxpayer's tax return. If more monies are needed to support individual political candidates, whatever amount Congress and the president feel can *reasonably* be allowed the taxpayer to donate to political candidates can be determined and stated on each taxpayer's tax return.

- **Lobbyists**

Lobbying is protected by the United States' Bill of Rights First Amendment. That amendment protects the rights to free speech, assembly, and the petitioning of government. In the case of lobbying, the First Amendment protects the lobbyists' rights to petition Congress to pass or defeat legislation that lobbyists represent, be they corporations, unions, religious organizations, or other groups. The lobbyists serve as those associations' advocates.

Because of the vastness and complexity of this country's government, there appears to be a definitive need for legislative help. Lobbyists fulfill that need. They both research bills for Congress and plead Congress for bills, as well as assisting the Congressional staff and Congressional members in preparation for the presentation of bills at Congressional hearings, where they may also testify for or against bills. They may even attend the committee meetings with Congressional staff and members of Congress.

It is obvious that lobbyists can and might be intricately involved in the whole legislative process. Because of the intricacies and immensities that are involved, lobbyists appear to play a vital part of the legislative progression in helping Congressional members do the "people's business."

However, there is a caveat. The lobbyists' involvements in helping Congress decide on the fate of particular legislative bills are not without risk. For they enter the legislative arena with a bias, a definitive prejudicial belief of why bills should be passed or defeated. That is how lobbying can work for or against the people's business, where *all* the interests and concerns of American citizens are being heard and responded to.

Therefore, it's my belief that lobbyists, whose job is to represent special interests, have become too powerful and have undue influence over Congress in either opposing or passing legislation more favorable to the special interests they represent—like corporations, labor unions, religious groups, and other moneyed alliances—than to what is best for America as a whole.

A 2009 article by David T. Cook of the *Christian Science Monitor* noted that there were 12,552 professional lobbyists striving to influence Congress on behalf of special-interest groups. In 2008, lobbying was a $3.4 billion industry. For example, Cook notes, "Washington tailor Georges de Paris sells suits that range in price from $3,500 to $25,000 and says 80 percent of his business is with lobbyists."[61]

We must remember that lobbyists are not elected nor do they represent the people, but rather, the special-interest groups that *hire* them to protect their interests, be they corporations, labor unions, religious groups, or other groups with a common concern.

Even though lobbying is a regulated industry, it is easy for lobbyists to influence legislation through bribery—using money, gifts, or other perks—or any other means to influence legislation. Measures to prevent such offences from happening, such as campaign-finance-reform legislation, is often promised but rarely passed.

What is also a bit troubling, is that when legislators lose reelection or choose not to run again for office, they often find a second career as a highly paid lobbyist. Obviously, this puts them in a decided advantage to have legislation passed favoring their particular interests, since they can meet with their former colleagues and tout the positions they are paid to promote, which, in some instances, may be positions they supported while in office. Even though such practices may appear illegal, an abuse of one's former position, this practice is quite legal.

The illegality may come when unlawfully large gifts are given to lawmakers or quid pro quo payments for votes—or this for that of some sort—takes place. However, such arrangements are hard to prove and easy to avoid through loopholes big enough to fly a private jet through.

---

61 http://www.csmonitor.com/USA/Politics/2009/0928/how-washington-lobbyists-peddle-power.

Since 1998, 43 percent of the 198 members of Congress who left government to join the private sector have registered to lobby, using the revolving door of influence.

Based on the track record of how lobbyists have performed over the years, it doesn't look like those previous members of Congress who became lobbyists did so with the thought of enhancing the lives of all Americans, as it is *assumed* they chose to do when they became members of Congress. But rather, the reason they choose to become lobbyists is for the financial reward. It's a bonus that they also get to continue work for and protect their own and various industrial and organizational political interests they had when they were Congressional representatives.

It's very easy to understand, then, how lobbyists can allow their lobbying pursuits to spill over into illegal and corrupt activities and practices.

According to the Bureau of Labor Statistics' online *Occupational Outlook Handbook, 2010–11 Edition*, "As of March 2011, the median annual salary for lobbyists is $98,652, with the top 10% earning more than $170,462." According to the bureau, "The average annual salaries of lobbyists will differ greatly on location, education, experience, employer, and type of work they do." Clearly the amount of money paid to lobbyists annually is anything but pocket change.

These salary statistics suggest that lobbyists might not have the best interests of their fellow American citizens at heart when they urge their Congressional partners to veto or pass a bill; but rather, they wish to advance their organizations' agendas, even at the expense of the common wishes and desires of the American taxpayers that Congress is supposed to represent. Further, that's a violation of the Founding Fathers' intentions, when they included in their Bill of Rights, the First Amendment right of freedom of speech, to assemble, and to petition the government.

It is clear that Congress needs to legislate certain safeguards to prevent lobbyists from running the government at the expense of Congress doing (We) the People's business as they were elected to perform.

In defense of the need of them, lobbyists Myers and Associates state on their website, "In many cases, lobbyists serve as an 'extension' of a Congressional office staff. Given the hundreds of bills and amendments introduced during each legislative session, it's impossible for legislators to gauge the potential effects that each may have on affected groups or individuals. Lobbyists assist staff by communicating often complicated issues and by knowing how to break an issue down into relatively small and simple parts. The goal is to simplify the learning process of the member and/or Congressional staff person, yet provide them with accurate and timely information. In this regard, lobbyists perform a valuable service not only to their client but to the staff and members of Congress as well."[62]

The caveat here, of course, is that if the Congressperson and his or her staff can't wade through the complications of a bill, how equipped would they be to separate the interests of the lobbyist and his or her client in the legislation from his or her advice about its benefit or harm to the American people?

According to the *Wikipedia* entry "Lobbying in the United States," attempts to regulate lobbying have resulted in The Lobbying Disclosure Act of 1995 and the Honest Leadership and Open Government Act of 2007, both of which increased regulation and transparency. In 2009, President Barack Obama signed two executive orders and three presidential memoranda on his first day in office governing how former lobbyists can be employed in the government, and restrictions on lobbying once leaving the government, suggesting he was aware that the power lobbying exerts in determining legislative decisions had gotten out of hand. Perhaps he believes lobbyists have taken governance out of the hands of the legislatures and put it into the hands of the corporations, unions, and other special-interest groups. I certainly believe that's true.

Still, I don't know of any legislation that will enable Congress to distinguish what will primarily benefit the lobbyists, their clients, and the Congresspersons who do their bidding and what will benefit the American people overall. What law can make sure Congress acts out of integrity and not out of selfish interest? That would require frequent and deep Congressional soul-searching and self-reflection, the members continually

---

62 Meyers and Associates. "Lobbyists and Lobbying." 1996–2007. http://www.meyersandassociates.com/lobbyist.html. (4 Sept. 2011).

asking themselves, *Do I want to pass this legislation to benefit the American people, the lobbyist and his client, or me?* Whether or not Congress chooses the American people always boils down to a question of ethics and how Congresspeople see their function of serving their nation. Do they want to do what's best for themselves or their nation?

I urge future elected officials to be vigilant in maintaining a hard-line stance in remembering that they have been elected to serve the people not the lobbyists. Realizing lobbying is protected by the right to petition, which is part of the First Amendment to the United States Constitution, it can't be eliminated, but it must be sufficiently regulated so that our system of government is not hijacked by those special-interest groups that the lobbyists represent.

Besides mitigating the power of lobbying, significant campaign-finance reform would level the playing field, because each individual campaign contribution would be limited and competitive. *If we had term limits, the politicians would not be thinking of capturing the vote in the next election and, therefore, would be more honest with themselves and the voting public.*

Furthermore, term limits might also free Congress members from feeling beholden to lobbyists, and therefore make them less inclined to support projects and other special-interest concerns that in good conscience shouldn't be supported. With respect to the House seats, lengthening the term served to be equitable to the Senate term could also reduce the possibility of campaign-finance abuse. On the other hand, it's possible that the person without a useful skill might be using his or her one term as an entry level position to the lobbying industry.

CHAPTER 12

THE POLITICAL PARTY VS.
THE AMERICAN PEOPLE

The Constitution provides the means to make what's wrong, right with this country. The Congress has the power to do what's best for all Americans. We can therefore deduce that when things don't go as planned, political malfeasance is the reason things have gone awry and why we as a people can no longer say, "I'm proud to be an American."

Compromise Is What's Required

The solution is for Congress to be willing to compromise and to put aside selfish interests for the greater good. Congress acts as if it's a helpless pawn in being able to adequately fight for what it thinks is right for America. Politicians like to constantly hammer home to anyone who will listen that it's the other guy who's responsible for the problem, not them. But politicians are part of the problem since they seem to have sworn their allegiance to their parties first and to the American public second. No wonder Congress seems so stalemated that nothing gets legislated. When they took their oaths of office, these elected officials swore to *protect and defend the Constitution,* which was written by, for, and of ... that's right, "We the People." But as long as they use their political parties instead of the Constitution as their political play book, the status quo will never change.

The Democrats are for a strong federal government to meet the needs of all Americans.

The Republicans are for limited central government to ensure that the rights and freedoms of all individuals will not get trampled upon.

They're both right, but neither party is correct in trying to reach their objective if they try to use extreme measures to do so, because they will never be willing to compromise.

How to Remedy the Situation

In order to get bills passed in both houses of Congress, it's the responsibility of Congress members to enter the arena of public discourse with a spirit of cooperation. That can only happen if all members view being elected to Congress as the honor and privilege to serve their country.

If members of Congress feel either for or against a bill prior to the vote for it, it's up to those members to use their political powers of persuasion to convince the opposition the error of their ways. As far as the American public is concerned, the only acceptable and legitimate way of debating the bill's merits is by members of Congress using their integrity, empathy, and compassion rather than party politics. They should come together in a spirit of cooperation and goodwill. Only by leaving their political armor at the door can they have an honest and vigorous debate of the bill's merits and ultimately come up with happy compromises satisfactory to both sides of the aisle. If that happens, we all win, and our country is all the better for it.

Candidates for Congress and the presidency must be up to the challenge of making the choice to seek political office not to receive power, prestige, and fortune, but because they are motivated by the strong passion and desire to respond to the needs of all Americans regardless of race, color, creed, political affiliation, socioeconomic status, sexual preference, etc. The fact that we're all Americans should be enough incentive for each elected politician to serve his or her country in the best way possible. In addition, what this country has to offer all Americans should be an added incentive to serve the nation, and by doing so, help make those dreams we each have for ourselves become realities.

One last point, in order to cover any future political contingencies—in addition to eventually passing into law all of the amendments I've mentioned in the previous chapter, we could start off on the right foot by establishing clearly that the reasons for passing the amendments in the first place are to *maintain a level playing field* for every citizen and to establish a sense of fairness and egalitarianism between our public servants, the politicians, and the people they serve, which is the American public.

The initial law that should be passed—the Twenty-Eighth Amendment—would prevent Congress from making laws that apply to the citizens of the United States but do not apply *equally* to the senators, representatives, president, and cabinet members, and likewise, Congress shall make no law that applies to them, that doesn't *equally* apply to the citizens of the United States.

More specifically, the Twenty-Eighth Amendment to the United States Constitution would state:

> *Where applicable,* Congress shall make no law that applies to the citizens of the United States that does not apply equally to the Senators and/or Representatives of Congress, the President, all members of government, appointed officials, and the like; conversely, Congress shall make no law that applies to the Senators and/or Representatives, Congress, the President, members of government, appointed officials and the like, that does not apply equally to the citizens of the United States.

By Congress and the president passing all the amendments I mentioned earlier, and getting them ratified by at least three-quarters of the states—the number needed to ratify a constitutional amendment—we will have again repositioned our nation to go down the tracks our forefathers would approve of. Our politicians would have once again acted like statesmen and stateswomen, and like our forefathers, set the stage where compromise is possible, and in so doing, allow "We the People" the opportunity to enjoy life, liberty, and the pursuit of happiness as stated in the Declaration of Independence once again.

CONCLUSION

I developed a real love for our Declaration of Independence, our Constitution, and our Bill of Rights as I studied them in preparation for writing this book.

Tragically, those documents are not as popular today as when they were written in the 1700s. Ever since the early 1950s, it seems that the beauty and significance of the words that filled those superb, handwritten pages diminished in importance and respect with each passing year. By the time we entered the twenty-first century, we had not only left our eighteenth-century awareness behind us, but we also left behind something that not only we, but other countries as well, revered and loved, which was our nation's integrity.

In addition to our nation's sense of wholeness, unity, and basic honesty, our country's fundamental goodness as expressed by Americans' storied empathy, compassion, care for and love of one another, and all those qualities that represent our individual souls was in part left behind as well. Because those were the endearing and enduring qualities reflected in our great charters, with these qualities' disappearance went the importance of what those three documents meant to each of our lives. The clarity and importance of those virtues have seemed less evident with each changing season.

The beauty of those three documents was in their simplicity and understanding of what our citizens stood for. That's why we need to respect those credentials as much as we honor one another. For it involves not only loving others but loving country as well, because our country's identity is derived from how we view ourselves and each other. Each document by itself represents a piece of our identity as a nation. Together, they not only represent our nation's identity but our collective, individual identities. The greatest gift we can give one another is ourselves and the love we feel toward our country and one another as fellow citizens of it.

The mainspring that made victory possible in the Revolutionary War, the Civil War, WWI, and WWII was the ability of us as citizens to pull together as a community and work toward something greater than ourselves—the creation and preservation of our nation. Whether they were a politician, fellow citizen, or part of the military, because they had a sense of purpose, their mission was clear and unambiguous—to defeat the enemy. The implied message they gave each other was uncluttered with political jargon and ambiguity. It was during those times when they had a greater sense of purpose in their lives. The mantra was *E Pluribus Unum* or "Out of many, one." They recognized the importance of common values and that the greatest joy comes from relationships. They were better able to empathize with and feel compassionate toward one another, because they were more other-centered then, compared to now.

Worthy of reflection: if you'll recall, I mentioned that after WWII, or the ending of the war on May 8, 1945, the United States citizenry was at its zenith in terms of feeling other-centered, working toward something greater than themselves, and being willing to give up their treasures and even their lives to protect their freedoms. That selfless and willingness to sacrifice all prevailed, even after their freedoms were secure. The reason that was so was because those of that generation simply knew it was the right thing to do. At that time, we had a lot to be proud of in being part of this great country we call America.

However, by the early 1950s, it seemed we began to start taking our eye off the proverbial ball, and we began to become *self*-centered, more insular, even to the point of only being concerned about our friends and family, most certainly not strangers or mere acquaintances. It was then we became less patriotic, less empathetic and compassionate, and more narcissistic.

As you might expect, while all of what I described was happening, our nation's integrity began to disintegrate in a parallel fashion. That was to be expected, since our country's integrity is simply a reflection of how our own morals and principles have eroded more and more over every passing year. As a result, we take our freedoms more and more for granted, and with that, we become more impulsive and live for the moment, rather than continue to live our lives in a purposeful and meaningful way, where we consider others as the center of our attention and concern, rather than ourselves.

What was the benchmark that caused us to move in that downward spiral, where we no longer regard our country in the way our brothers and sisters, the colonists, felt about our nation when the Founding Fathers wrote those magnificent documents, the Declaration of Independence, the Constitution, and the Bill of Rights, the principles and dictates of which have stood the test of time, and where each person who reads those documents can ultimately say, "I'm proud to an American"?

The benchmark that prompted this downward spiral might have been when, in the 1950s, Congress changed our motto to, "In God We Trust," to differentiate us from the "ungodly Communists." This motto, was subsequently put on our money and added to the Pledge of Allegiance, but was not part of the founders' impulse at all. My sense is that as soon as God replaced The People as the unifying force, things started to go south. Now, we don't even remember the feeling of "Out of many, one," or *E Pluribus Unum*.

Let us remember how the Founding Fathers, with their diverse interests, beliefs, and backgrounds, were yet able to come together and set aside their selfish interests and petty concerns for the good of their country and future generations, and were able to write those three marvelous documents. Their effort was, in and of itself, quite miraculous. The fact it was accomplished at all, speaks of their cooperative spirit, selfless natures, and their wanting to do something that was indeed, greater than themselves.

Knowing that, perhaps our Founding Fathers were centered in the *pluribus* part of *E Pluribus Unum*, the *many* part of "out of many, one." Considering the singleness of purpose that this diverse group of patriots embraced, they were eager to make their many voices a single call to purpose and destination, which was how to maintain their country's freedoms.

Because of the replacement of *E Pluribus Unum* as our de facto motto with an official "In God We Trust," our politicians became either centered in God or not centered. *To me that's a travesty and a pretense, and it may have damaged us to the core.*

Much earlier, when our nation's citizens were filled with patriotism, the reason the Declaration of Independence, the Constitution, and the Bill of Rights had stood the test of time and were revered by not only Americans, but also many other people around the world, was because what was enunciated and clearly spelled out in those documents were elements that comprise bits and pieces of the integrity of each of us, Americans and foreigners alike.

There are many differences and similarities between us all, whether we choose politics for a living or any other livelihood. However, one thing we all have in common is our integrity, or that part of our being that makes us feel whole and undivided, truthful, authentic, and uncompromising. Let's look at that for a moment.

Throughout the book, I've talked a lot about not compromising your principles and, in that sense, *never compromising your sense of integrity.* Further discussion is necessary because I can see where some confusion may arise concerning these words. Since no two *integrities* are exactly the same, but are all different, because they are all based on each of our unique life experiences, there can be differences in the way we each express our integrity, and we can each be correct. However, at a deeper level, our integrity is the same, because when we violate our sense of it, at that level, we've violated a moral stricture that we, as Americans, all believe is important to live by.

What I'm talking about when speaking of having an uncompromising sense of integrity are those beliefs that have a moral or ethical undertone to them, where *what you do* violates your belief system in one way or another, so much so that your integrity is compromised.

Assessing whether or not you've violated your moral code is situational. That is, if you're a politician and you're duplicitous by telling your electorate that you're going to do something they wish done, but because there's a bigger political gain by not doing that and doing something else, so that's what you do, you are being duplicitous, dishonest, and two-faced, because you've violated your sense of integrity or honesty.

What do you want from your leaders when the negotiating gets tough? Do you want them to work for consensus while getting some of what they campaigned on passed by Congress and made into law? Or do you want them to fight for what they campaigned on, holding firm to their ideals? Obviously, if they did the latter, they would be acting like our current Congress is acting, and no compromise would take place. On the other hand, in order to keep the business of government operating optimally, so bills get passed and made into law, getting *a little* of what you want in order to achieve a satisfactory compromise, where you don't sacrifice any of your ideals and values or your principles (ethics) is what politics should be all about. When you can achieve a happy compromise where bills get passed and made into law for the good of all the people, then government is operating as it should.

By getting in touch with our integrity, we learn what's important to us, and we become able to respond with empathy, compassion, love, and caring for others. Simply expressing such feelings makes our lives worth living.

The political climate today has become more strident and discordant. We, as a country, have become more insular and narrow-minded. Instead of being other-centered and helping others, we have become more narcissistic and self-serving, and we have become less tolerant of views different from our own.

As I mentioned earlier, in order to get in touch with our souls, or where our integrity is housed, along with all the other values and virtues that make us human and our lives worth living, we must periodically stop and reflect on what we, as Americans, should be all about. And when listening to politicians tell us what to do with our lives, we should begin to question whether or not what they say about our country and our fellow Americans is what we *should* be concerned about. If we look hard, we might start expecting our leaders and ourselves to place greater credence and value on living with integrity, empathy, and compassion. All of which are the same kinds of values and virtues that many of our Founding Fathers held dear to their hearts. If politicians did that, they would start getting in touch with what really matters in our lives, rather than continuing business as usual and letting such values and virtues take a backseat—making it easier to act for the good of the politicians' parties or their political agendas rather than the people now and in the future of the country.

By engaging in business as usual, the politicians continue to brainwash us into thinking that the most important thing in our lives is to get them elected or reelected so that they can continue to provide us with vacuous and self-serving pursuits—all done to make more money for themselves and their party and the few who have bought them at the taxpayers' expense. Now that's not what our democratic republic should be about, is it?

In order to bridge the schism that exists between and among Americans as well as between political parties, we need to reacquaint ourselves with the Declaration of Independence, the Constitution, the Bill of Rights, and the other seventeen amendments. For the message that's contained in each of those documents are words we should live by.

The Founding Fathers wrote those documents for the common man— "We the People." That was done so that everyone in the new country and all the generations hence would understand what the important factors in a democratic system are, and how democracy's weaknesses can be addressed with a republican form of government. The documents were kept brief and general so that we *as a people* could understand what we should consider when we think about how to approach ourselves and others as a self-governing nation.

Importantly, the Founding Fathers did not write those documents in an emotional vacuum. Considering the political climate of the time, the events leading up to the war for independence, and the colonists' actions that precipitated the writing of our nation's democratic maps—there was ample emotional stimulus to prompt their inscriptions.

Yet, I wonder if politicians of today reading those documents—if they read them at all—receive them with any emotion or passion. If they do read them and let themselves imagine what it must have been like to live through that period, realizing that the future of the country rested on what the Founding Fathers wrote down in those documents, surely it must stir some feelings of patriotism. If they do that, they would more likely put America's citizens' best interests ahead of their petty politics and personal needs. They would avoid the political mess we find our nation in today.

Since emotions frequently precede thought, it is important for politicians to recognize the feelings they might be experiencing that trigger their thinking. That's assuming of course their thoughts are not only about themselves, but *our* sense of well-being and happiness as well. By being able to reflect and understand themselves, they will be able to develop both their private and public virtue, and responding with empathetic and compassionate understanding, do what's best for not only themselves, but more importantly, our nation's health and preservation as a whole.

Passing those amendments as suggested in chapters 11 and 12 is the first step in getting our politics on the right track where politicians return to serving the people rather than themselves. But their responsibilities do not end there. It is important for the *new* political statesmen and stateswomen to begin to study the history of this country and to *viscerally* understand why the Founding Fathers viewed serving their country as being an honor and a privilege, why they were willing to be part of something greater than themselves, in order to fight against tyranny within and without.

The only way we as a nation—politicians and nonpoliticians alike—can begin to put our country first, rather than our own selfish interests, is through education. We need to educate ourselves and our children about what the virtues are that maintain and preserve our democratic system of government, and why that knowledge provides our republic with an ability to fulfill the demands that are enumerated in our living, sacred charters, and in that way, be able to fulfill the mandate of serving *all* of America's citizenry.

We must begin to accomplish that goal by doing what our country's founders urged us all to do, and that was to develop courses in our classrooms explaining why and how our system of government came to pass and why the colonists were willing to sacrifice their treasures and even their lives to protect the freedoms proclaimed in the Declaration of Independence and then clarified in the Constitution and the Bill of Rights.

The subject matter of those courses should capture the wisdom of that period, and the famous personages of that era should be generously quoted. In so doing, it should be thoroughly understood why what they wrote had relevance for them and continues to for us today as well. By better understanding the history of that period and why those documents are so special, we can then begin to understand how we as a country have failed to instill more of that wisdom and political acumen into the psyches of our citizenry. When we are able to do that, instead of continuing to be passive participants in the political process, we will be able to actively honor our allegiance to our flag and our country. Because, as the founders knew, it is through knowledge and critical thinking, not blind loyalty, that we can hold onto the wisdom of that revolutionary period and fulfill our nation's destiny as envisioned by our forefathers.

* * *

I've learned much about what's important in my life by writing this book. One of the conclusions I've come to is that we, as a country, have lost sight of what's of value in this world. It's not money, power, or fame that will make our lives complete, because if we use any of those criteria as a standard, we're never going to be fulfilled. We'll always have a feeling that our lives are not complete, and we will continue seeking more of the same, like an addict reaching for an elusive and false state of nirvana.

But if we want to be able to say, "I've lived a full and complete life," rather than valuing money or material things, power, or fame, we need to value our relationships—our immediate family and others that we love and care for, as well as our relationships with our communities, our relationships with all our fellows.

When all is said and done, if we knew our days were numbered and we reflected on what was most important in our lives, we would know what was important. That's why when loved ones die who meant so much to us, but we never realized how much, we regret never having told them how dearly we loved them before they died.

On the other hand, when losing those people whom we consistently treat with love and compassion, expressing our respect for them the whole time we know them, we might grieve for their loss, but last-minute regrets are few and insignificant. The reason is that those people knew you loved them, because that's how you consistently related to each other when they were alive. With love, empathy, and compassion.

Starting with our parents and other people we meet in our journey through life, we all have models that we want to emulate and become. Although the unconscious searching for those kinds of people becomes less apparent as we grow older, nevertheless, identifying with those we admire and love continues throughout our lives. The reason we do this as soon as we're born is because we wish to compensate for our innate feelings of inferiority. We feel inferior because everybody around us can do things better than we can. This compensation for real or imagined feelings of inferiority is what we do from the time that we're born to the time that we die. The older we become, the less urgent and imperative the searching for an adequate role model, because with age comes experience, knowledge, and wisdom, all which adds to our competency quotient. What all of this personal discovery has done for me is to make me realize the importance of introspection or reflection, integrity, empathy, and compassion in each of our lives.

The same is true on a national or political scale, and politicians who strive to emulate our Founding Fathers, even now in the twenty-first century, could make a giant step forward in doing what's necessary to make this country whole again. Of course, we would all do well to learn about the lives of our Founding Fathers; certainly the benefits of taking on their level of character and integrity would be worthwhile to incorporate into all our personalities, but it would be of special value for those who wish to serve their beloved country as politicians, whether it's at the local, state, or national level. Because if there is ever a time when integrity, empathy, and compassion needs to be present, it's when you enter politics. These qualities are the mortar or the glue that holds the political thoughts together and helps the politician not only *appear* credible, but also to actually *be* credible in service to *all* Americans and not just a political party.

Private and public virtue, which include empathy and compassion, are still cornerstones of our great nation. We need people who serve because they want to do something for their country, not because of potential reward of fame, fortune, or power, but because they want to give back to their country what they have so generously received. We need people who are willing to take a stand and tell the truth, even if it is unpopular. In short, we need statesmen and stateswomen who know that securing the blessings of liberty is worth any cost—personal, monetary, or public.

When we as Americans, whether we are politicians or not, live our lives with integrity, empathy and compassion, and don't settle for anything less from others, ultimately, we're going to say with pride and love in our heart, "I'm proud to be an American."

EPILOGUE

I grew up during World War II. My father was too old to join the military, but in his own way, he was very patriotic. He believed in supporting the war effort by buying war bonds and doing anything else to help defeat the Axis powers: Germany, Japan, and Italy. He said that if he were younger, he would gladly join the service and give up his life to safeguard America's freedoms.

He believed that the Constitution was the greatest document ever written, and that Benjamin Franklin was the greatest American who ever lived. As a creative engineer, I think he admired Franklin because of his prowess in the natural *engineering* of ideas. That's because Dad earned an engineering degree from MIT and, like Ben Franklin, loved inventing and creating things.

I believe if he had studied our Founding Fathers as I have, he'd recognize there were many people of that era to admire and claim as men of history to admire, but if he were to put aside all his prejudices and biases, he'd conclude the greatest man of that era was George Washington, "The Father of our Country."

When I was a young teenager, my dad asked me and my two older brothers who we thought was the most famous person during the Revolutionary War period. I was at a loss of what to tell him, since I didn't know anything about that period in our American history. I knew nothing about our Founding Fathers, because I had never had an American history class in school, or if I did, sadly, I didn't remember anything about the subject. But that question prompted my curiosity about that period in history from that time forward.

My father was always a strong influence in my life. I accepted what he said at face value, because he said it with such conviction. As a result, I've always had a deep love of country and what it represented to me, believing that America symbolized all that's good in the world. Recently, however, I discovered how very broken our system of government is today.

By the time I finished writing this book, I felt uncomfortable about what our country had become compared to how I viewed it growing up. The difference felt stark and severe, since what I saw was so contrary to what I believed our country should be all about.

Up to when I started writing, I didn't fully realize the importance reflection, introspection, and empowerment plays in each of our lives. It's tremendous. That's because by reflecting on our lives and investigating our thoughts, we begin to understand what's important to us and what kinds of thoughts move us to action. We can only feel moved to act, however, if we also feel empowered, having developed a degree of confidence, to understand why we think as we do and whether or not our thoughts are important enough to share with others, so they too will be moved to action.

Well, that was exactly what happened when I wrote *What Would Our Founding Fathers Say?* Because of the passion I developed as I investigated our history and what I thought about it, I had no option but to become actively involved in the whole political process in a way I hadn't been before. Yes, I seem to have had an epiphany: If a country is to be *of the people, governed by the people, for the people,* then only *the people* can make that happen. And I am one of them.

If what you're doing is not taking responsibility for your country's political future by becoming more involved in its political process, I think it's important to change that. We must all become more responsible for our country's political destiny. Rather than passively following the so-called *herd mentality* and trying to avoid being more actively involved politically, the first step is to start to connect with the political process itself: you need to become more politically knowledgeable.

164

Reading this book is a start. But beyond that, make sure you are familiar with the principles and tenets of the Declaration of Independence and the Constitution and Bill of Rights, and not just accepting what media pundits say about them. These amazing documents can only be honored and revered as they were when our Founding Fathers established our fledging nation if we understand what's in them—not what they symbolize to this one or that one, but what they actually say. Then you might read about what the men who crafted them had to say about them, rather than accept what today's political players *say* they thought. Our nation's original builders have never been so accessible to us as they are now. You can find almost all their writings and letters and actions online.

Empowerment is what authorized me to act and behave as one of the people invoked by the words "We the People" … That was the real-world payoff for all the work I went through to get this book into print. I sought its publication because of the deep concern I felt for our country. I feel we're headed in the direction of certain destruction if we, *as a nation of free citizens,* don't change our government to more accurately reflect what our Founding Fathers intended our country to be.

What a sense of empowerment does for each of us is it gives us a greater sense of confidence or self-esteem that we didn't necessarily have before. When you feel empowered, you have no choice but to act upon your new sense of positive regard, even though it may be but a whisper in the political world of public opinion. You feel compelled because of the long hours of thought and research you've put in to arrive at the conclusions that you did. Armed with understanding forces you to stand up and be counted if you feel there's even a remote chance that your shared thoughts and ideas will influence public opinion and help get our country moving in the right direction again.

I would imagine that many politically uninformed, naïve Americans must feel like I once did—impotent to change the system in the ways it needs changing. In order to avoid a feeling of apprehension, they steer clear of thinking about political issues of any kind. That's because if they allowed themselves to think of alternative ways of dealing with the political problems of the day, different from how they've thought about them for years, they'd only end up feeling more helpless, confused, and anxious. That's because of that old demon *cognitive dissonance*—there are so many conflicting and diametrically opposed points of view out there, when you listen to all the various parties engaging in political discourse, it is hard to adopt a view contrary to what you have grown up believing.

So it's a natural tendency to avoid dealing with, *or even thinking about,* politics altogether. It's just as natural, if you think about it at all, to grasp onto the same old hackneyed reasons for supporting one party over another. But these choices are just efforts to maintain the status quo and avoid cognitive dissonance to keep anxiety at bay. It's a good thing our Founding Fathers did not make that choice, natural or not.

Or maybe your reason for not being more open-minded to differing views or solutions is because no one likes to acknowledge to others, let alone to him or herself, that perhaps he or she was wrong in what he or she believed was true for so many years. Isn't that why religion and politics are not to be discussed in public? Those are two subjects that many of us hold dear to our heart. To acknowledge that perhaps we made a mistake in either one of those two subjects would be too much to bear.

Not that your current viewpoint *would change* because of further study and discourse; a changed one is not necessarily any more valid than your existing one. That is not the point. It's that you have an opportunity to arrive at your conclusions after some study and musing, rather than in knee-jerk fashion. That alone will provide you with considerable solace and peace of mind; politically based cognitive dissonance does not stand a chance once you feel empowered in politics. You will then *welcome* political discourse and discussion, because you've looked at all sides of the issue.

On the other hand, you pay a price for being uninformed, and that is a feeling of impotence and inferiority when you compare yourself to those who are more politically savvy than you are. These people can then manipulate your opinion for their own gains and hidden agendas that have nothing to do with you. But the acquisition of knowledge gives you a feeling of authority and enlightenment, a powerful combination when it comes to being able to talk about politics in a self-assured and confident way.

The impulse to speak out when your sense of integrity is being threatened is as right and real in the field of politics as it is in any other subject that you're passionate about. But only when you can consciously stand the bare facts against your own preconceptions (there are those public and private virtues again) can you trust that your need to defend your beliefs against that which runs contrary to them is the right thing to do and not just an avoidance of apprehension.

There are many times in our journeys through life when we must act a certain way or make our voices heard, even under great harassment and persecution—if it's not the sanctioned or popular thing to do at the time. However, if what you have to say involves your sense of integrity and might influence the course of the discussion in a positive and constructive direction, then you owe it to yourself to make your voice be heard, regardless of the consequences of your actions.

One last word. At this point in the writing of this book, I feel so proud and accomplished, almost special, privileged maybe, in ways I have never felt before when thinking about *politics*. In that sense, I feel I have *come of age*. You see, I had something to say that I felt was important and that I believed would make a significant difference in people's lives, and I said it. Because I want "We the People" to once again be able to say, "I'm proud to be an American."

BIBLIOGRAPHY

Adams, John to Mercy Warren. 16 Apr. 1776, Warren–Adams Letters 1:222–23 in Kurland, Philip B. and Ralph Lerner, eds. "Epilogue: Securing the Republic," chap. 18, doc. 9, *The Founders Constitution.* http://press-ubs.uchicago.edu/founders/documents/v1ch18s9.html.

Blomfield, Adrian. "Israel delivers ultimatum to Obama on Iran's nuclear plans." http://www.telegraph.co.uk/news/worldnews/middleeast/iran/9121433/Israel-delivers-ultimatum-to-Obama-on-Irans-nuclear-plans.html. (3 Mar. 2012).

Bureau of Labor Statistics. *Occupational Outlook Handbook, 2010–11 Edition.* 2010–2011. http://www.bls.gov/oco/. (11 Nov. 2011).

Burnett, Bob. "The New American Revolution: Occupy Wall Street." *The Huffington Post,* 21 Oct. 2011. http://www.huffingtonpost.com/bob-burnett/the-new-american-revoluti_b_1023748.html. (28 Feb. 2012).

Center for Responsive Politics (OpenSecrets.org). "The Money Behind the Elections." 2010. http://www.opensecrets.org/bigpicture/. (28 Oct. 2011).

Chernow, Ron. *Washington.* New York: The Penguin Press, 2010.

Conte, Christopher. "The US Economy: A Brief History," in *An Outline of the U.S. Economy*. U.S. Department of State: http://usa.usembassy. de/etexts/oecon/chap3.htm. (15 Jul. 2012).

Creech, John. "The Classical, Liberal Arts Education of the Founding Fathers." Centerfortheamericanrepublicblogspot.com. 8 Apr. 2011. http://centerfortheamericanrepublic.blogspot.com/2011/04/classical-liberal-arts-education-of.html. (1 Mar. 2012).

Donald, David Herbert. *Lincoln.*New York: Simon & Schuster Paperbacks, 1995.

Gilson, David. "The Crazy Cost of Becoming President, from Lincoln to Obama." motherjones.com. 20 Feb. 2010. http://motherjones.com/ mojo/2012/02/historic-price-cost-presidential-elections. (29 Feb. 2012).

Historic Documents. "Bill of Rights and Later Amendments." ushistory. org. 1995–2011. http://www.usconstitution.net/consttop_pre.html. (4 Sept. 2011). http://www.ushistory.org/documents/amendments.htm. (4 Sept. 2011).

Kertscher, Tom. "Political vitriol is bad these days, but experts say it's been worse" politifact.com. 16 Jan. 2010. http://www.politifact.com/ wisconsin/article/2011/jan/16/political-vitriol-bad-these-days-experts-say-its-b/. (11 Mar. 2011).

Kurland, Philip B. and Ralph Lerner, eds. "Epilogue: Securing the Republic" in *The Founders Constitution*. John Adams to Mercy Warren, 16 Apr. 1776, Warren–Adams Letters 1:222–2. http://press-pubs.uchicago. edu/founders/documents/v1ch18s9.html.

Levinthal, Dave. "Congressional Members' Personal Wealth Expands Despite Sour National Economy." OpenSecrets.org. 17 Nov. 2010. http://www.opensecrets.org/news/2010/11/Congressional-members-personal-weal.html. (20 Sept. 2011).

Lincoln, Abraham. "Letter to Horace Greeley," at Abraham Lincoln Online: Speeches and Writing. http://showcase.netins.net/web/creative/lincoln/speeches/greeley.htm. (05 Jul. 2012).

Lyke, H. John. *The Impotent Giant.* Bloomington, IN: iUniverse, 2007, 2008.

McGrath, Jane. "10 of the Biggest Lies in History. Bernie Madoff's Ponzi Scheme." 1998–2012. http://history.howstuffworks.com/american-history/10-biggest-lies-in-history3.htm. (26 Feb. 2012).

Murse, Tom. "The Citizens United Ruling: A Primer on the Landmark Court Case." About.com. http://uspolitics.about.com/od/firstamendment/a/Citizens-United.htm. (6 Jul. 2012).

_____. "What Is a Super-PAC?" About.com. http://uspolitics.about.com/od/firstamendment/a/What-Is-A-Super-Pac.htm. (4 Mar. 2012).

_____. "The Wealthiest Members of Congress," About.com. 2012. http://usgovinfo.about.com/od/usCongress/ss/Wealthiest-Members-of-Congress_3.htm.

Meyers and Associates. "Lobbyists and Lobbying." 1996–2007. http://www.meyersandassociates.com/lobbyist.html. (4 Sept. 2011).

Mount, Steve. "Constitutional Topic: The Preamble." usconstitution.net. (24 Aug. 2010).

Poliska, Kelli. "The Cost of Running for President." datacraftrockford.com 24 Sept. 2008. http://www.datacraftrockford.com/blog/bid/27985/The-Cost-of-Running-for-President. (29 Feb. 2012).

Revolutionary War and Beyond. "The Purpose of the Declaration of Independence." *Revolutionary War and Beyond.* 2008–2011. http://www.revolutionary-war-and-beyond.com/declaration-of-independence.html.

Rosenberg, Jennifer. "Vietnam War" About.com. 2012. http://history1900s. about.com/od/vietnamwar/a/vietnamwar.htm. (5 Mar. 2012). http:// usa.usembassy.de/etexts/oecon/chap3.htm.

Tradingeconomic.com "United States Economic Rate." http://www. tradingeconomics.com/united-states/unemployment-rate. (2 Feb. 2012).

Washington, George. "Valley Forge Encampment: A Winter of Suffering." http://www.cr.nps.gov/logcabin/html/vf.html. (27 Jul. 2012).

Wikipedia. "Enron Scandal." http://en.wikipedia.org/wiki/Enron_scandal. (26 Feb. 2012).

_____. "List of federal political scandals in the United States." http:// en.wikipedia.org/wiki/List_of_federal_political_scandals_in_the_ United_States. (10 Mar. 2012).

_____. "Lobbying in the United States" en.wikipedia.org. 15 Feb. 2012. http://en.wikipedia.org/wiki/Lobbying#United_States. (4 Mar. 2012).

_____. "Monica Lewinsky." http://en.wikipedia.org/wiki/Monica_ Lewinsky. (27 Feb. 2012).

_____. "Watergate Scandal." http://en.wikipedia.org/wiki/Watergate_ scandal. (26 Feb. 2012).

Worldsavvy.org. "What is Democracy." worldsavvy.org. Aug. 2008. http:// worldsavvy.org/monitor/index.php?option=com_content&view=artic le&id=183&Itemid=297. (3 Mar. 2012).

ADDITIONAL READINGS

Aziz, Robert. "Why Power Corrupts and Absolute Power Corrupts Absolutely." huffingtonpost.com. 2011. http://www.huffingtonpost. com/dr-robert-aziz/why-power-corrupts-and-ab_b_920638.html. (4 Sept. 2011).

Kelly, Martin. "Causes of the American Revolution." About.com. 2011. http://americanhistory.about.com/od/revolutionarywar/a/amer_ revolution.htm. (1 Sept. 2011).

Lexrex.com. "An Important Distinction: Democracy versus Republic." lexrex.com. The American Ideal of 1776: The Twelve Basic American Principles. http://lexrex.com/enlightened/AmericanIdeal/aspects/ demrep.html. (1 Sept. 2011).

National Archives and Records Administration. "Marshal Plan." archives. gov. 3 April 1948. http://www.archives.gov/exhibits/featured_ documents/marshall_plan/. (4 Sept. 2011).

National Bureau of Economic Research. "Business Cycle Dating Committee, National Bureau of Economic Research." nber.org. 11 Dec. 2008. http://www.nber.org/cycles/dec2008.html. (4 Sept. 2001).

Wiki.answers.com. "Did George Washington command in the French and Indian Wars? wiki.answers.com. 2011.

———. "What is public virtue?" 2011. http://wiki.answers.com/Q/What_is_public_virtue. (4 Sept. 2011).

Wikipedia. "Boston Tea Party." Wikipedia.org. 30 July 2011. http://en.wikipedia.org/wiki/Boston_Tea_Party. (1 Sept. 2011).

———. "George Washington in the French and Indian War." Wikipedia.org. 11 Aug. 2011. http://en.wikipedia.org/wiki/George_Washington_in_the_French_and_Indian_War. (7 Sept. 2011).

———. "Olive Branch Petition." Wikipedia.org. 25 June 2011. http://en.wikipedia.org/wiki/Olive_Branch_Petition. (1 Sept. 2011).

———. "Shays' Rebellion." Wikipedia.org. 24 Aug. 2011. http://en.wikipedia.org/wiki/Shays%E2%80%99_Rebellion. (1 Sept. 2011)

———. "United States Constitution." Wikipedia.org. 31 Aug. 2011. http://en.wikipedia.org/wiki/United_States_Constitution. (1 Sept. 2011).

CPSIA information can be obtained at www.ICGtesting.com
Printed in the USA
LVOW041223220912

299820LV00001B/2/P